MUSIC by MELICK

FAMOUS IN CERTAIN CIRCLES

70 Years of Big Band Memories
(and the Beat Still Goes On)

JACK MELICK

COMPILED AND EDITED BY

Nick LaVecchia

A *Music by Melick* Book

THEWRITEHOUSE | PARKER, TEXAS

This *Music by Melick* edition is an original publication. It is published by arrangement with the author.

Published by THEWRITEHOUSE
5407 Kara Lane, Parker, Texas 75002

Manufactured in the United States of America

ISBN 978-0-9974085-0-8

With loving memories, absolute respect, and total admiration, I dedicate the writing of this memoir to my beloved grandfather; William J. (Pop) Stryker. He played the violin and cornet and was an inspiration to me every day of my life until he died when I was 17 and away at college. I still have his cornet.

My mother, Marjorie B. (Margie) Melick, nee Stryker, was my hero and remains so to this day. None of the events described in this book would have happened if not for her love and inspiration (i.e., "It's time to practice, Jack."). She made my life special and I often sent letters to her from various spots in the world, thanking her for everything.

A special mention should be made of Maestro Joseph C. Schaedel. He was my music teacher in grammar school and my band-directing guru in high school. He was a great man and an inspiration to all of the music-minded kids who came in contact with him. None of us will ever forget The Old Maestro!

Jack Melick, 2016

"Living in Dallas, Leslie Ann and I divorced after 9 years. I went over to visit the kids one afternoon, and my youngest, Mandy, who was about 6 or 7 at the time, came running out to me. She seemed excited, and said something like, 'Daddy, are you famous?'

'Well, why do you ask?' I replied.

'I heard your music on the radio today,' she said. That was true. It was being played around this area anyway.

'Well, let's see,' I said. 'I'm famous in a way... with a certain group of people mainly... let's just say I'm **famous in certain circles**.'"

Jack Melick

Contents

Foreword

The first time I saw Jack Melick was in 1952 at the Club 45 N.C.O. Club in Yokohama, Japan. He was standing on stage emceeing a variety floor show. He had a mike in one hand and a beer in the other. My first thought was that you shouldn't be drinking a beer on stage. Today, if you don't have a drink on stage, you're not working. We had an immediate dislike for each other and have been close friends ever since.

Jack has always had multiple interests in life. Music is #1. He knows about all the artists of the Big Band era. He's a student of politics, economics, and has one of the most fantastic memories that I have come across. He's especially brilliant in remembering names, Japanese or American, and can recall jokes and material performed by comics 30 years ago. I have trouble remembering what I did last week.

And, of course, the ladies. Not having romance in your life is like having a band without a piano— which makes no sense at all.

A musician's life is difficult. Jack always worked mostly fronting his own band. Reno, Vegas, Texas. His children all graduated from college and are successful today.

I starred with Anthony Newley in the Broadway-bound musical *Chaplin*, the life story of Charlie Chaplin. Luckily, the music for one was minimal. I played Chaplin understudy Stan Laurel.

I remember Jack telling me when he started taking piano lessons, his mother said, "Practice 15 minutes a day. That won't kill you." Soon, he was up to three hours a day.

There are no shortcuts in life.

He tried to help me with my music. He started me out on the cowbell—banging the cowbell to the beat. He said practice five minutes a day. I could only practice two minutes a day. The noise was killing me. Then I progressed to the spoons. Clicking two spoons together. Finally he said, "Maybe you don't have God-given talent." And we laughed. I said the spoons were too small. He gave me teaspoons. For real sound, you need tablespoons. And we laughed.

To me, our friendship was more than what we did for a living, and we've kept in close contact through the years. When I call him, or he visits Southern California, it's as if no time has elapsed since the last time.

Jack is traveling and fronting the last of the big bands. And he is helping thousands of older folks remember the good old days while dancing to some beautiful timeless standards and listening to some good music. Some very, very, very good music. When you work hard and have good friends, it all adds up.

Jack usually got the girls, but I got the laughs. You tell me which is better.

Jim MacGeorge, 2015
Comedian, actor, and performer in the Jack Melick Show

Preface

I've never been out of work. When I would finish (or lose) a job, I immediately got another one. Every place I've gone to play, I've always gotten along with the manager, even when the managers were really bad people! They always brought me back. Some of the jobs we play now are in places we started playing 40 years ago.

Some of my guys, like Wes Smith, Mark Roberts and Marshall Head have been through it all with me; some for more than forty years.

So, how could we fail? The answer is, we couldn't.

Of course on the road there were times that were tough, maybe not all that wonderful and exciting. I know, I was on the road for decades. So people will ask, "Why did you do it?"

Drinking cold coffee from a styrofoam cup in the middle of the night in Iowa, Nebraska, Kansas, or parts unknown...

Trying to sleep in a noisy old bus...

Leaving after a dance and traveling 400 miles to the next gig...

Sleeping in a ratty old hotel (two guys to a room no less)...

Away from home and family for months at a time...

Working in a smelly worn tuxedo because there was no stop that week long enough to do laundry...

Eating bad chili with a half inch of grease on top on the road in the middle of the night...

Why did we do it?

It was the music.

Yes... it was the music.

People have asked me for years to write down all my stories. So, a friend and I finally decided to do it. Of course, no "kiss-and-tell," just my musical thoughts and memories from the Big Band era to now, in Texas. I hope you enjoy the journey with me.

1
A Kid From Jersey

You Know What Kind of a Year That Was

Hackensack, New Jersey is in the northeast part of the state just across the Hudson River from the Bronx. About 40 miles to the southwest is the town of North Plainfield, New Jersey where I was born, and where I grew up. I've never lived in Hackensack, so it was always strange that my dad called me "Wacky Jackie from Hackensacky" when I was little. I guess it was the only New Jersey town he could think of that rhymed with my name.

He also used to say, "Yes, Jack was born in 1929, and you know what kind of a year that was..." He thought that was real funny. Me, not so much. But despite the notable financial meltdown that year, 1929 turned out to be an okay year for the Melick family.

I was born John T. Melick, Jr., and I have been known as Jack all my life; Jackie when I was little. Since my dad was the first John in the family, we had to know who the calls were for when the phone rang, so they started calling me Jack real early, and it's been Jack all the way.

North Plainfield was just a normal "small" town to grow up in, but we were only 22 miles from Manhattan. I caught a bus two houses down on the corner to go into New York City and hear the bands starting when I was 10 or 11. I have to say that as a kid who wanted to play music for a living, I was pretty lucky to live where I lived because all the greats came to New York—Louis Armstrong, Dizzy Gillespie, Duke Ellington, Charlie Parker, Count Basie, Stan Kenton,

Harry James, Sammy Kaye, Freddy Martin, and I could go on and on. I got to see them all.

Some of my childhood stories are probably only interesting to me. But they're straight from the musical culture of the 40's and 50's—the Great American Songbook as we call it. This is what we knew when I grew up, and I think you have to understand a little bit about where I come from to get all the rest. So I promise, the Hollywood stories are coming up. If you want to skip ahead, you're more than welcome!

The Neighborhood

I guess what I remember most are the field across the street where my friends and I played ball, piano lessons, and the names of the girls in the neighborhood—not necessarily in that order. Yep, let's see.... Eleanor Boerner lived next door. Carol DiVico was down the street. Behind us was Ava Rita Riley. Frances Kentner lived behind us also and so did Clara Silsby.

Don't ask me why I remember the girls so well. I guess it's one of the stereotypes of male itinerant musicians that happens to be true. There's an old Duke Ellington anecdote that also occurred to me throughout my career as early as my teen years. (Duke said that this continued all his musical life too.) I think I was about 13 when I started to notice that when I'd be playing piano somewhere, I'd look at my left hand and standing by the left side of the keyboard would be a pretty girl. So needless to say, I knew that music would be in my life really early. Of course, today the pretty girls are a little bit older. Ok, so they live in a retirement community, but there's still one always standing there when I start to play. Duke told me that he experienced the same thing as a young man.

I remember the field across the street mostly because I spent so much time there playing ball with my friends. Other than music, baseball was a great love of mine too. One of my favorite stories involves the great Stan Musial. Did you know he played the harmonica? Well, I'll tease you with that one for later. And let me clear up another misconception right away. Those that know me personally know I have a cat named Stan the Man. As much as I liked the legendary St. Louis Cardinal, my cat is named after my idol Stan Kenton.

But the field also led to the one time I got in serious trouble with my mother. For lack of anything better to do, my buddies and I set the field on fire. (The statute of limitations has run out by now on that, hasn't it?) We thought that was pretty funny because we sat on my porch and watched the field burn. But my mother figured that one out, and she wasn't very happy with us.

There are many other childhood memories I won't bore you with—ice skating with the girls (again with the girls), fishing in Green Brook, mom's homemade root beer, and summers at Point Pleasant Beach on the Jersey shore. Mostly, I remember the piano lessons. Those other things are left behind as childhood memories, but the piano lessons sort of stayed with me.

Can't Remember Life Without Music

As early as four or five years old my parents put me in front of a piano. I think at the beginning they just did it because that's what you did. You gave your kid piano lessons. My mom was a musician herself, and she was very good on the piano. She even played for the silent movies in 1917 and 1918 on Sunday nights. I would say she knew pretty quickly that I liked it and was going to be fairly good at it.

I didn't like to practice much when I was a kid, but what little boy does? She asked me to practice only 15 minutes a day, but it had to be every day. She'd sit next to me on the piano bench and we'd concentrate for 15 minutes. She believed that a kid can do something he doesn't like for 15 minutes a day and it's not gonna kill him. Many a day, the guys were outside waiting to play ball, and they sat on our porch for that 15 minutes and waited for me to come out. She limited my practice (but kept it consistent) so I didn't get to hate practicing. And so that's how I started out, and music has now been my life's pursuit for about 80 years. I said I wanted to be a big band leader at age 6 or 7.

So as you can tell, my mom was a very important childhood influence musically, but I'd also say there were two more.

My maternal grandfather was a very accomplished musician, and he and I spent many hours together doing duets—me on the piano as young as 6 or 7, and him on his violin. William J. "Pop" Stryker was a shoemaker by profession but he played the violin and the cornet. The violin is long gone, but I've still got the cornet. It's a little over 160 years old and it holds an honored place on my mantel. My mother got her musical talent from him. He and I were really good buddies and I would go and stay with him for two or three weeks in the summertime, and then he would come and stay with us for the winter. Mom didn't mind my three weeks away. She used to say, "Jackie may not brush his teeth and he may have corn-on-the-cob for breakfast, but I know he'll be safe with Pop Stryker."

When I started to play a little better, he taught me to play Stephen Foster melodies—Old Black Joe, Suwanee River, Old Dog Tray, Camptown Races, stuff like that. He would play the violin or the cornet, and I would play the piano. He liked a good cigar, loved music, and loved to tell stories. So I come by it honestly—well everything but the cigars.

The third influence on me was my high school band director—Maestro Joe Schaedel. He was a great man and a good friend of my dad's. They both belonged to the Kiwanis Club. Of course, I'm thinking ahead a bit, but I knew I wanted to be in the marching band in high school. Well, I found out you can't march with a piano, so we decided I would learn to play the clarinet, which you can march with. We got a $35 all-metal clarinet. I haven't seen one in ages, but I remember it cost $35. I started taking clarinet lessons in middle school from Joe Schaedel. That's when I first met him and became very close to him on a personal level. For the four years of high school, he was probably my most important musical influence. He was one of my childhood heroes.

But Dad, I'm only six!

Well I guess by now I should have mentioned that my mom's name was Margie. So one of the songs my dad wanted me to learn first was "Margie."

He said, "You've got to learn to play 'Margie' right now."

I said, "But dad, I'm only 6!"

Anyway, as soon as I was able, I learned to play "Margie" at my dad's request, and as a matter of fact, I guess I played it for her for about 80 years. I played it until she passed away at the ripe old age of 102 in the year 2002—maybe one of the few people to have been alive in both 1900 and 2000.

I guess you could say my dad was my original agent—both my parents really. They kept me busy showing me off to family and friends. I must have played well fairly early because my folks asked me to play whenever friends came over. At the age of 7 or 8, dad would occasionally take me to his favorite hangout—near the Prudential Insurance office where he worked, called Herm's Bar—and he would sit me up on the piano bench and have me play for the guys at the bar. All his co-workers were there late Friday afternoon. So I suppose that when they got off work, they'd stop for a drink at Herm's. He had me play the piano there when I was really small, but I have to admit I really liked it. There were no pretty 7- or 8-year-old girls at my left hand quite yet, but I got drawn into performing publicly pretty early.

Great Teachers

My first teacher's name was Mabel Whitman. Mrs. Whitman would come over twice a week. In those days you didn't go to the teacher. They drove around like doctors making house calls, and she came over to our house twice a week for a half-hour lesson. Again, mom thought that an hour was too long for a 6- or 7-year-old. So Mrs. Whitman came twice a week for a half-hour music lesson.

She was a very nice lady. She was not hard on me. Actually she was probably too easy. My mom often said she wasn't a great teacher, but the way she taught let me enjoy what I was doing. So in that sense, I guess she was a really great teacher. She was probably 60, but you know how that is—it's hard to tell how old someone is when you're a kid.

She taught me classical music, and provided me with the fundamentals—what note to hit when you see a certain mark on paper. I think Mrs. Whitman came over for at least 7 or 8 years, right into my high school years which is the time I met a musician we all knew as Doc Brown.

Earl "Doc" Brown taught me what I wanted to learn—popular music. And by "popular," of course, I mean the Big Band sound and the Great American Songbook. So I guess all of us together—my parents and me—decided that I would start taking lessons from Doc Brown, but not stop with Mrs. Whitman who was teaching me "legitimate," or classical, music.

At the time I was taking popular music lessons from Doc Brown, I went to his place because I was old enough to ride my bike or take the bus on my own. You know, not that he would have made house calls anyway. Actually, Doc Brown was "legally blind." He could see, but not well. I had to go down to the music store where Doc Brown was teaching in a studio upstairs. I would take a bus or ride my bike down there once a week and study with him. Doc taught me how to read chords, how to play what is called a "swing bass," and how to improvise on chords—all the stuff you need if you're going to play popular music.

Doc played in the lounge at the Park Hotel, a hotel in

Plainfield, on the other side of Green Brook.

By the way, another guy taking lessons from Doc Brown was one of my friends and classmates at North Plainfield High. His name was Bill Evans. We called him Billy. When Doc Brown would have a recital of his students, he would have me play something by Chopin or Schubert, and he would have Billy improvise on something like "Body and Soul," "Embraceable You," or "I Only Have Eyes for You." Even as a young teenager, he was already a very fine jazz pianist. Billy had more to do with the direction of my career than anyone else. More on that a little later.

I studied with Doc Brown and Mabel Whitman until I went away to college.

Of course, my third great idol was Joe Schaedel. Besides teaching me how to march and play the clarinet, I suppose, he taught me a lot about being the leader of the band—what it means to organize and lead. My college degree is in public school music, inspired mostly by Joe Schaedel. I figured if I couldn't make it as a dance band musician, I could always teach high school band. I first went to college as a piano major. When I got out there I was exposed to all these kids that were prodigies. The Oberlin Conservatory of Music at Oberlin College in Ohio was one of the premier music schools in the country—still is. I heard some of these child prodigies play and I knew I couldn't play that well and never would. So I switched to music education with an intent of being a high school band director if my dreams of the big band world fell through.

In my senior year of high school, Maestro Schaedel became very ill and had to leave school. They made me the band director from the beginning of school in September until sometime in the spring when he came back. So I felt like this is what I was supposed to do, because even in high school I was "the leader of the band."

I remember one time we had to go to Cranford, New Jersey to play in a parade. That morning it looked really nasty outside, but no rain was coming down. I called the school superintendent in North Plainfield, Mr. Bare, and asked him if I should order the buses or call it off.

He said, "Jack, whatever you do is going to be wrong. So take my advice and don't worry about it."

I said, "Gee thanks," called the buses, and we went down. Well, I knew what he meant. I was the leader, so it was my job to make the decision. Make the call, and then don't second-guess yourself. Well, it never did rain. We marched in the parade and got a medal for second place. My band mates thought I was great. As I recall, they cheered for me on the bus on the way back. It was an experience and a lesson about leading the band that I've never forgotten.

Joe Schaedel remained a good family friend and followed my career even into my Dallas days. He was a mentor and supporter right up until the time he passed away.

The Musical Culture of America

Of course if I was born later, I might have focused on rock-and-roll or whatever. Whatever was going on, I probably would have wanted to do it regardless of when I was born. But our music was the music of the Great American Songbook. (You can go ahead and look up Great American Songbook on the Internet if you wish.)

My dad took me to the Cotton Club to see Louis Armstrong. I was very young, but that just did it! THAT was music. That was the musical culture of the country. These "golden years" lasted only about 25 years, but it was the musical culture of America. As we were growing up, we followed our favorite bands, and we knew all the musicians' names that played in those bands.

Who played lead alto with Harry James? We knew who it was.

Who played tenor sax, and who played the drums for Stan Kenton? We all knew who it was.

All that was just the culture, and if you were a music student, you knew all about it. That was my friends and me. We all knew a guy in Plainfield who played with Benny Goodman. And we thought, "Wow, how do you get to play with Benny Goodman?" His name was Jerry Jereminski, but he changed it to Jerry Jerome. He played tenor sax with Benny Goodman, Glenn Miller, and Artie Shaw, and we all knew about it.

There was a family in Plainfield that had three sons who became well-known musicians and played in the big bands, and we knew all about it. Bobby Van Eps, John Van Eps, and the most famous of the three brothers, a guitar player, was George Van Eps. When they left Plainfield, New Jersey and went on the road with these big bands—Bob Crosby, Benny Goodman, Artie Shaw—we all knew about it.

That was the music culture of the country and if you were interested in popular music, that's what you listened to. And something else about it—music in those days brought the family together. We didn't go off in different directions with our headphones and listen to our own music. We didn't even have headphones or recorders! We all listened to this music together in our homes and it filled the whole house from the radio or the phonograph. There wasn't the separation of the generations that occurred in the rock-and-roll era. Parents and kids all liked the big band music. Sure, there were different styles. In general, older folks liked quieter dance music, and a lot of us younger ones liked jazz music, but it was all still the big band sound.

Now That's Big Band Music!

There used to be a Sunday night radio program that we listened to every week called the *Fitch Bandwagon*. It was sponsored by Fitch shampoo (another one you can look up on the Internet). A different band was on the show every week, and they would broadcast from the city in which that band was performing at the time. I remember one time we were listening and Freddy Martin's band was on. They were very famous at the time and they were playing "Paper Moon." My dad said, "Man, that's a band! That's a real band!" Well, I couldn't have imagined it, but about 20 years later, I was in Freddy Martin's band and the same version of "Paper Moon" was still in his arrangements.

So that's when it started, and we listened to big band music on the radio all the time. My Aunt Eleanor lived with us for some years. Every day, when she came home from work, she'd tune the radio to *The Make-Believe Ballroom* with deejay Martin Block. It was on every night, and it was a two-hour show. She'd sit there the entire time and listen to the whole thing.

Aunt Eleanor often took me to the Paramount Theater in New York to see a big band show and a movie. The movie started at 10:00 and the band would come on at noon. Then the movie would start again at 1:00 and the band would come on again at 3:00. This went on all day. The Paramount was famous because that's where they started dancing in the aisles when Benny Goodman was playing there in the 30's. The Capitol and Strand theaters did the same thing. We'd go to hear Orrin Tucker's band. He had a vocalist who became very famous. They called her Wee Bonnie Baker. She had a little hit number called "Oh, Johnny."

Anyway, I sat in the audience and watched Orrin Tucker's band and I was just enthralled with it. Just like Freddy Martin, many years later I would be in Orrin Tucker's band. In fact, I played with him for two years as his featured pianist. But here he was, on the Paramount Theater stage when I was a kid, about 11.

Louie Prima and his band were playing at Frank Dailey's Terrace Room in Newark when I was still in high school. My mom and dad took me and my girlfriend to hear them. His singer was a girl named Lily Ann Carroll. I went up to talk to Louie Prima during a break. Big gawky teenager that I was, I had my big saddle shoes on as I stepped on the stage and walked past Lily Ann Carroll. She was wearing this long, flowing, netted gown. So I stepped on her dress and ripped the netting about half way around. Those big dumb size 12 saddle shoes... I was so embarrassed. I apologized profusely and she said, "That's okay honey, I'll go back to the dressing room and fix it." I'll never forget how nice she was to me.

Another time, at the Strand in New York City. I was about ready to head off to college. Sammy Kaye's band was playing. When the movie was over, the band would be set up on the orchestra stage in the basement, and a hydraulic lift would bring them out of the bowels of the theatre, so to speak, up to main stage level. So, after his hour was over, I went down the aisle when the orchestra was coming down again, and I stepped onto the stage, which had come down to floor level.

I said, "Mr. Kaye, I'm graduating this year. I play the piano. Where do you suggest I go to school?"

He said, "It doesn't matter. Listen to your teachers and practice."

The orchestra stage continued on down and I stepped off and went back to my seat to wait through the movie (again) to catch Sammy Kaye one more time.

A Day at the Theater

My friends and I eventually figured out how to stay in the show all day. We'd get in for the first show at 10:00 or 11:00am. We'd find seats wherever we could get them. At the end of the movie, people leave. When they'd leave, we'd move down. We had a brown bag of sandwiches with us. We'd watch the band show and then the movie again. When the movie was over the next time more people would leave. By the third or fourth show—I remember we stayed all day—we were down to the front row. One Saturday Count Basie was playing. I'm sitting there on the front row, and up comes the orchestra stage on the hydraulic lift, and there's Count Basie and his band. They're playing "One O'Clock Jump." Oh my gosh, they were right above me.

So, halfway through the show he introduces his guest star for that day, the legendary Billie Holliday. Billie Holliday came out and was right up there; right above me in a white dress and that signature white gardenia in her hair. She's up there singing with a voice I will never forget. It took all day to get to the first row, but it was worth it.

We'd take a lunch and go on a day like Columbus Day when there was no school and stay all day. We had to watch that darn movie three times in order to get close to the band sometimes, but that's another great experience from the big band era that just doesn't exist anymore.

Birdland

The jazz musicians were really my heroes, you know, because it was just so hard to play jazz, and almost impossible to make a living at it. All of us who were making a living doing what we called "commercial music" would go hear Dizzy Gillespie or Charlie Parker or Stan Kenton play when we had a day off. We always liked jazz because of its creativity.

Birdland in New York was named after Charlie Parker. He was also known as "Yardbird" or simply "Bird."

Birdland was for music lovers only. There was an area where there was no cocktail or food service. It cost a dollar and a quarter. (Imagine trying to get into a concert today of the best music you ever heard for that amount of money.) You'd go in and sit there and listen to all these great musicians. The rest of the place did have tables and tablecloths where people were going to have dinner or a drink. But, for a dollar and a quarter college kids and high school kids could go in and sit there in the "music lovers section" and just listen.

One time I was sitting in Birdland listening to Charlie Ventura, I think, and there's a girl sitting next to me, a young African American girl. She's singing along with the band, and it was Sarah Vaughan. By then she was already pretty well known, and there she is. She had come in to hear the bands too. There was this great voice singing along with the band. You know, this kind of stuff just happened all the time.

So You Want to Lead A Band...

Sammy Kaye did a special number in all his shows he called "So You Want to Lead a Band?" He'd bring people out of the audience, give them a baton (which he had signed), and let them lead the band. The band would start playing, the audience member would stand in front of the band and lead it. Sometimes it'd be pretty funny.

Well, Sammy Kaye's band was playing at the Adams Theater in Newark. I went up on stage when the contest came up and told Mr. Kaye that I wanted to be a band leader. There were three of us that volunteered that night. He asked me if I wanted a "fast one or slow one." And I said a fast one. He probably thought, "Well, we've got one who thinks he knows something here."

Anyway, he turned around to the guys and said, "One O'Clock Jump." I stomped my foot eight times—when I was that young I counted eight beats before the band came in to play instead of the normal four—and they came in on time and played the "One O'Clock Jump." There I was, still in high school, leading Sammy Kaye's band in "One O'Clock Jump."

Well, I won that night. My reward was a $50 war bond and that signed baton. I still have it—the baton that is.

That was a great time. I was at the age when I could pretty much go wherever I wanted on my own. Newark was only a few miles from where we lived. As I wrote earlier, I took the bus just down on the corner from my house. Now, there was a burlesque theater near the Adams, too—the Empire. I would usually tell my mom I was going to the Adams Theater to hear Woody Herman or someone like that. Of course, I wasn't lying. I did do that, and then maybe I'd slip over to the Empire Burlesque with the guys. Of course, we went there just to hear the funny jokes. You know, we didn't go to see the girls or anything.

A full afternoon of girls—wait, I mean *jokes* and music. You couldn't beat it.

Jack Melick and His Orchestra

When we got to the age where we could play fairly well, we wanted to form a band. Today they're called "garage bands," but in New Jersey we all had basements. Our bands were called "basement bands." At age 13, we started my first dance band. By age 15 or so, we were playing paid engagements as "Jack Melick and His Orchestra." That's the way bands were billed at that time—Tommy Dorsey and His Orchestra, Benny Goodman and His Orchestra. I was probably a little ahead of myself, but it sounded just great to me!

We played at all the important high school dances. We're in the mid-1940's at this point. The war was on. Like Korea a few years later, circumstances put me and my friends in the right place at the right time. Again, I don't want to seem grateful for war, but we got a lot of good professional work because the war was on. All the older musicians had been drafted. And so a bunch of us at the young ages of 14-17 were playing dances for the Elks Club, the Knights of Columbus Club, high school proms, or wherever they wanted a dance band. It was an opportunity we never would have had. There may have been a few exceptions, but professional musicians were much younger than usual because the older guys were in Europe, North Africa and the Far East.

We played a lot of USO shows. In fact, I played the piano for a tap-dancing class on Saturday afternoon; Doris Mae's dance studio. It was my first paying gig at the age of 14 —50 cents an hour—and we would tour with the students from her tap-dancing studio at Camp Kilmer and other military bases. We were just kids; me the 14-year-old wily veteran at the piano and Doris Mae's kids dancing for the troops before they left for war.

So I learned at an early age a lot about playing in public and playing for singers. A lot of the songs I learned then, I still play now. Good memories and great overall professional experience way earlier than I normally would have gotten it. We grew up fast in the music world.

In the summer of 1946, Jack Melick and His Orchestra got a job in the Pocono Mountains to play all summer. We were all 15 or 16 years old at the time, but these summer resorts were hiring high school kids because there weren't any other young musicians around. We played at a resort called Camp Sagamore; popular big band dancing every night and square dances on Thursday. (I had to learn to play square dancing music.) We played amateur night shows on Friday. The guests put on the show, so I had to learn how to transpose and accompany vocalists. I would get a little nervous during rehearsals. Somebody would come up and say, "I want to sing 'Old Man River' tonight." And I'd say, "what key?" and hope that I could play it in that key. But it was all part of the gig, you know. That I remember as being the hardest part; transposing.

Of course, it wasn't all music. We had to sweep the ballroom every morning, and on Saturdays we had to carry baggage. Saturdays was a popular arrival day for weekly stays, and we'd carry the bags at check-in. I always wondered if any of the guests did a double-take at the show that night after seeing us all carry in their bags that afternoon! But we got our weekly pay plus room and board. And I was a big band leader working in the Big Band Era!

The guys in the band got $20 per week, and I got $25 a week because I was the leader. I was 16, and I had to learn how to lead a big band six nights a week in a real venue. I experienced the same issues any big band leader would. I had an argument once with my drummer. During the break I said, "Well, let's be pals. Come on. I'll buy you a drink." Now we were both 16, so I bought him an orange juice. My drummer's name was Geoff Edwards, and like a lot of the personalities you're going to read about, he became famous in much larger circles than I did. He became a well-known TV reporter and popular game show host.

Anyway, we played at Camp Sagamore for three summers. Even after I went to college, I came back the summer after my freshman year and played our third year.

You might be wondering how my parents felt about all this. Actually, I'd say they were probably pretty proud. They would show up often on Saturday nights, but they never told me when they were coming. The Sagamore stage faced the dance floor and beyond the dance floor was the entrance. So as I'm on stage playing or leading, I'd look out there and my mother and father would be coming in. Sagamore was only 80 miles from where we lived. They would come often to see what their "little boy" was doing. Even in subsequent years, they would show up unannounced just to make sure I was behaving myself. They came to Houston, Dallas, California, Reno; everywhere I was playing, at least in the United States.

I don't think I could have asked for more supportive parents. They were always there. Even from the beginning. When we were real young, my mother would stay up and make hamburgers for the band. We would all come back to the house after we finished a job, and she'd be up to make hamburgers for us. And you know, it was a big band, so there were lots of mouths to feed.

Bill Evans

Bill Evans became a world-renowned jazz pianist. He won 7 Grammys and was considered one of the greatest jazz pianists of all time. And he was the reason that I became the leader of the band. When any of the bands around town had local jobs, they would call Bill Evans to play piano for them. We call that person a "side man." I couldn't get a job as a side man, and I couldn't get a job as a side man because Bill was called first. He was the guy.

One of my first jobs was playing with a band from Plainfield. I played one engagement with them at the Dunellen High School prom. Dunellen was a town nearby. I was only 13 at the time and felt pretty good about myself and Tony Gatti, the leader of the band, told me that I did a good job, but they were going to replace me with Bill Evans. I realized that this was going to happen a lot as long as we were living in the same town. I figured then that the best way for me to get work was to form my own band. That way, I didn't have to depend on someone else to hire me. I thought I was a natural leader anyway. My parents agreed and encouraged me in that direction. I was not nearly the jazz player and improviser that Bill was, but I knew good dance music, good dance tempos, and knew that this was the way for me to pick my own tunes and count off my own tempos. Besides, how else could I pick the songs that I wanted to play?

I think it all worked out. I don't know many leaders who have played big band music better than we have. It's just about all I've ever done and I've never tired of it. I've always loved it. Yeah, those piano lessons sure stuck with me, all right. I've made a living, and a comfortable one at that, doing what I love. I feel like the luckiest guy in the world, and I feel like I have never gone to work in my life.

2
College and Lifelong Friends

A Campus College Life

When it was time to look at colleges, my parents and I talked about them all. Of course, Eastman and Juilliard were at the top of the list. Both were well-known conservatories. Eastman is upstate New York in Rochester. Juilliard, of course, is in New York City. But my mother, who had been guiding me in most of my music choices, said, "Well, I think you should have a top-notch music education, but I think you should also have a campus college life."

Juilliard, Eastman or the Curtis Institute in Philadelphia, which was another one we liked, were urban schools. They had no campuses. You'd live in a regular apartment, take a bus or street car to class and go home after school and that was it. She wanted me to have a college life also.

About 20 miles west of Cleveland is the small town of Oberlin, Ohio. The Conservatory of Music at Oberlin College is probably not as well known as Juilliard, but is certainly comparable in terms of the quality of the education and the musicians it graduates. And it turned out to be a great place to continue the education of John T. Melick, Jr. Oberlin College had about 2000 students when I attended there, and only about 400 in the Conservatory. It's not much bigger than that today. It turned out to be a great move. My best friends today are still friends I made at Oberlin. I went home Thanksgiving, Christmas and summer, had a normal college life, and learned music at the same time.

I Had to Audition First

Well, unlike most college disciplines, musicians have to audition to get in—at least at the top music schools. For admittance to the Oberlin Conservatory, you had to audition and sit for an in-person interview. The Director of the Conservatory at that time, Mr. Frank Shaw, came to New York to Carnegie Hall studios for those reasons. Mr. Shaw accepted me because he thought he saw some musicianship there; the possibility of developing this kid into something. My high school academic grades were average, but my music grades were all A's!

I went to Oberlin Conservatory of Music as a piano major. When I got out there I heard other students in the practice rooms playing. And I'd hear them at student recitals. I'd listen to these guys and girls play the classics. And I was not that good, and knew I would never be that good. Some of these prodigies would practice 8 hours a day or more, and that's all they knew. I was never that deep into it. I wanted to play music and make a living at it, sure, but I was always interested in other things too. When I practiced three hours a day; that was plenty!

Of course, I didn't want to be a concert artist anyway. Everything I had done to that point was aimed at becoming the leader of a dance band. When I arrived at Oberlin, I arrived as a piano major. But it didn't take long to figure out my best bet was in public school music education. Like I wrote before, one of my heros was my high school band director. I wanted to be prepared to be a band director because I admired Joe Schaedel and I admired his job. If I never made it in the dance band business, I could definitely see myself as a high school band director. Well, I received my degree in public school music education, but of course I never used it.

I Learned a Lot of Songs

I still had one more summer to go on my three-summer deal at Camp Sagamore after my freshman year. So this time, I took a couple guys from Oberlin with me to play there. When we went back to Oberlin for our sophomore year, I had a couple key players who had been with me all summer. That second year I built my Oberlin campus band around them. But more on that in a bit.

For three more summers after that, I went home and played alone in a bar down at Point Pleasant Beach on the Jersey shore. It turned out to be a great experience, but I only got it because I was fired from another job—the only time I ever lost a job because I wasn't good enough. Well, I did my best to make sure that never happened again.

Near the end of my sophomore year, I put an ad in one of the musical trade magazines: "Available for the summer. Can fake, read, sober. Have tux, will travel."

I got a call from a band leader in Pittsburgh. He said they were going to be playing that summer in West Virginia at the Cheat Lake Supper Club near Morgantown. They needed a piano player. He sent me a plane ticket and met me at the Pittsburgh airport. We drove from there to Morgantown, only about 75 miles.

That first night down there, we were playing for the first time. There were only five pieces, so there wasn't sheet music for anything. There was no rehearsal either. We just went straight to the job.

He says, "Zing, in F. One, two, three, four..." I had no idea what he meant! I just sat there and the other guys started playing.

Well, that was his way of saying, "We're gonna play 'Zing Went the Strings of my Heart' in the key of F." Well, I didn't know "Zing Went the Strings of My Heart." Then the tune "Josephine" came up. I didn't know "Josephine" either. In the middle of the first night he says, "Jack, uh, you don't have the experience to play with us because we play these old tunes and you're too young. You don't know them."

Well I learned that lesson well, because I have fired guys over the years since then, too, for the same reason. I didn't know a lot of the "old" tunes then. They didn't know the "old" tunes in my days as a leader.

So, I was fired by a real nice guy. If you're going to get fired, it might as well be by a real nice guy. His name was Al Freeman. He said, "Sunday, I'll drive you back to Pittsburgh. I'm going home for the day off, and I'll buy you a ticket home."

So he had me play the intermissions there for the rest of that week. I played alone. I knew how to do that, because I only played songs I knew. That's how I got through that week. I flew home, took the bus from Newark Airport back to North Plainfield, and knocked on my kitchen door.

My mother came to the door and said, "What are you doing here?"

"I got fired."

That was that. The family went down to the Jersey Shore for the summer, as was our summer custom, and I went down with them. Well, even the best can come from unexpected circumstances. I looked around down there for somewhere to play, and about 5 blocks off the beach, I found The Club.

The Club was a typical (for 1949 anyway) local beach hangout. They were looking for a guy to play the piano in the cocktail lounge. To my good fortune, I played there the rest of the summer. In fact, I played there two summers more. Playing alone, I learned a lot of songs and made lots of local friends. People would come in and make requests all the time.

An old Italian guy—who used to drink green beer—said he wanted to hear "Come Back to Sorrento." Well, I didn't know it of course, but I learned it. And someone else would want something, and then someone else. It went that way all summer. I learned "I Only Have Eyes for You" that summer. I learned a lot of songs on that job. So if I didn't know a song, I told them "I'll play it for you next time you come in." I built my library that way by playing alone in The Club.

A recent trip back home took me that way, and I went looking for The Club. It's still there sixty-some years later! The bar was still there, but the piano wasn't. I sat at the bar and a bartender came by.

"What'll you have?"

"A beer," I said. "You know I played here in 1949."

He said, "Oh yeah? What beer do you want?"

Young guy. He's down there for the summer too. College kid waiting on me. Couldn't care less that I played there about 60 years earlier.

I said, "The owner here now?"

"No, he's not here tonight."

That was my big welcome back to where I started my

career! I drank my beer and left.

Well, I made money for the summers of '49, '50, and '51. I met a lot of nice locals, and learned a whole lot of songs.

A Pretty Good College Band

That freshman year of college was the first year I didn't have a band since I was 13! I didn't know enough guys yet to form a band, you know, so I worked in the snack bar there in the student union to make my own spending money. My last summer in the Poconos included some of my new musician buddies.

I was always scouting around to form a band and I formed one for sophomore year centered around those guys I brought with me to Camp Sagamore in that summer of 1948. I had that dance band for the rest of the time at college. We played somewhere just about every weekend—all through northwestern Ohio. We went to play at a lot of the colleges in Ohio. We got a reputation around the "Ohio Conference" as it was called; this group of about 20 small liberal arts schools.

We played at Kenyan, Antioch, Wittenburg, Hiram, Wooster and others. We'd go down and play at a beer keg party, and then drive home to Oberlin. Sometimes, I wonder how we got back alive (kidding), but we'd get down there in the afternoon. By that time, the football game was over and the keg was opened. We could partake of the beer (sometimes that was our payment) and then play music. It was great.

An Unforgettable Night

At Oberlin College in 1948, no one was allowed to have a car unless you needed it to help pay for your education. I had a car because I had my band and needed the car to get us to our gigs. Well, having the car allowed a certain amount of freedom too. I remember one night when Stan Kenton and his band were playing in Cleveland at the music hall there. So, three or four of us decided we wanted to go hear Kenton's band. And that's what we did. And, it was wonderful.

After it was over we walked around the block and there was Kenton's bus parked by the stage door. Being college kids having driven all the way to Cleveland, we hung around the bus. Of course, eventually they all came out. The band members, and June Christy, his vocalist, all came out and we started talking to them. We were Oberlin students and they knew all about our school. They were really terrific guys. So we're talking to these guys and I think it was Milt Bernhart—Kenton's lead trombone player—who said, "We're going up to a club. It's called the Club Tijuana. Do you know it?"

We said, "No."

He said, "Charlie Parker is playing there tonight. We're driving up there to hear him. Why don't you come with us?"

I don't know what's faster; a New York second, or how fast we agreed to come.

Then I guess we thought we ought to be safe, and we asked Stan Kenton himself. He said, "There's no room on the bus, but you're welcome to follow."

The Club Tijuana was at 55th and Euclid—in the middle of Cleveland's ghetto at the time. It was a place we probably wouldn't have heard about, but Charlie Parker was playing there. We went in and sat at some big tables. They were really tickled to see Kenton and his band come in. We all sat there and listened to Charlie Parker. Miles Davis was playing the trumpet with him. This was before the years they became legends in music. But they were still giants.

And here we were. A bunch of college musicians, sitting with Stan Kenton's band listening to Charlie Parker and Miles Davis. That night goes down in my memory as being maybe the greatest in my life. In one night, I heard my favorite band—Stan Kenton—and then I heard the greatest jazz players in the world—Charlie Parker's band. Jim Lloyd, one of the guys in my group, was so excited that he went around and got every autograph in Kenton's band, including their wives! (There were 3 or 4 wives traveling with Kenton's band.) George Weidler was the lead alto player at that time; Doris Day's former husband.

That was some night. When I arrived in Hollywood in 1955, these guys were all around town, and I got to meet them all again. Bernhart remembered me, and so did a trombone player named Harry Betts who became a good, personal friend through the years out there.

Lifelong Friends

In those days, on a co-ed campus, the dormitories each had their own cafeterias. They also had a cafeteria on campus but I never ate there. I wanted to eat at the girl's dorm, with the girls and the guys that went there to eat dinner. Junior and senior year you could sign up at the beginning of the year to eat at one of the girl's dormitories. Dinner every night. There were eight of us that ate together my entire senior year. Somehow we just all joined up. We were four couples. And we all became real good friends.

We have a reunion every year now. There's actually still seven of us left. We have three days of telling stories about what it was like when we were together at Oberlin. There's the night that I drove up the dormitory steps in my car. Each year the story gets worse until it sounds like I drove into the lobby. That's the night when Al Weingold, Les Sherrill, and I came home from a game of canasta. They swear I drove up the Burton Hall steps to let them off at the door instead of on the street. I don't think so, but you know, musicians were weird even then.

One of the guys was a trombone player—Dick Strang. He wasn't in the Conservatory at Oberlin, but played the trombone. He played in the college bands but became a banker actually. Al Weingold became a doctor. I was the only one of the eight who became a professional musician. One of the girls that ate with us actually married a guy from the Conservatory who became a musician in New York. She's gone now, but he's still playing in New York even though he's old like I am. Strangely enough, I made most of my friends in the college as opposed to the Conservatory.

Stan Kenton

Stan Kenton was a piano-playing band leader which was just what I wanted to be. He had his own style and his band didn't sound like anybody else's band. It was loud and brassy. It was a swing band, and never played what we would call the corny type of ballroom music. Then later on, he experimented in different types of big band music. He was a very forward-looking guy. He had a band in the late 1940's and the early '50's that he promoted as "Innovations in Modern Music." He added a couple of French horns. He added additional percussion like bongo drums. I loved that band.

We'd have arguments at school about which band was the best band in the country. Most of the music students liked Woody Herman's band. He was great of course, but the rest of us were Stan Kenton fans. Woody Herman had more of a true swing band. I thought Kenton's band swung too, but he was also much more of an innovator. But reviewers always said he was interested in experimenting, that he dismissed the idea that these bands had to have a swing feel.

And of course, there was June Christy. Christy was a beautiful young woman who sang with the band, and every teenage boy in the U.S.A. was in love with her. And one of them got to sit right next to her and hear Charlie Parker play at the Tijuana Club.

3
Off to War and the Far East

"Greeting"

I knew I was going to be drafted. We all knew it. Other people were being drafted who were not in college. They waited for those of us who were in college to graduate. So when I graduated, I went home, went down to the seashore for my regular gig at The Club, and sure enough...

As I recall, the letter came in late July or early August.

The first word on my draft notice was (supposed to be) "Greetings." Only there was no "s" on the end of it. It said "Greeting." (The very first word on my draft notice was a typo!) On August 24th, 1951, I reported for duty to Camp Kilmer, New Jersey. My mother said she'd never forget what I looked like walking across the lawn to get in the car. She felt like she might not ever see me again. I don't know... I never thought anything about that. I didn't even worry. I just had to go because the draft notice came.

Basic Training

After induction, it was off to 16 weeks of basic training at Camp Chaffee, Arkansas. During the four months of basic training there, I went through regular training activities with everyone else. There was no music involved, of course. Just a lot of running and crawling and weapons training. But all the army service clubs had pianos, and on my own time, I played at the Camp Chaffee service club every chance I got. I found a job in nearby Ft. Smith at a joint called The Silver Spur and played there on Saturday nights—well, except for a couple

Saturdays when I didn't pass inspection or get a weekend pass!

Dick Strang, from Oberlin, had gotten to Chaffee a month before I did. When he finished, he went directly into the Army band at Camp Chaffee with the understanding he was going to be there for the rest of his two-year stint. Well he wasn't even a music major, so I was sure that I would go into the band there too! But something happened in Korea, because all the specialties were cancelled. No cook school. No leadership school. No band. Everybody was put into the enlisted pipeline for Korea.

That was in December of 1951.

Next Stop: Tokyo

Japan was supposed to be a place that I would only stay a few days before being assigned to a fighting unit in Korea. Camp Drake in Tokyo was what they called a "repositioning depot," or hub from where all soldiers were dispersed to their various units. Turns out, I would stay in Japan just a little while longer than a few days!

It was winter in Japan when we all arrived. I was issued my parka because it was real cold. I was issued an M-1 rifle, got it zeroed in, and was all ready to go. Unlike Camp Chaffee, however, there wasn't much to do at Camp Drake while waiting for your number to be called. Like I wrote earlier, I played piano wherever I could find one. So sure enough, there was one at the Camp Drake service club.

One night, I was playing the Fats Waller hit "Ain't Misbehavin'" in the service club. After awhile, a guy in uniform came up to me—no stripes, just a private like me—

and he said, "You play pretty good. Are you based here?"

"No, I'm in the pipeline to Korea," I said.

"Well, we'll have to see if we can't do something about that."

Of course, here's a green private just like me, so I looked at him and figured he'd had too many beers or whatever.

Well, the next day proved that you can't judge a book by its cover—or in this case—a private by his lack of stripes. I got a call from the director of the army band in Tokyo, the director of Special Services in Tokyo, the director of the army band in Yokohama, and the director of Special Services in Yokohama, all asking about my musical background and experience. It turned out that the director of the 289th Army Band in Yokohama was an Oberlin grad. Warrant Officer Brown asked if I might be interested in being in an army band and I said, "Well sure, because I'm on my way to Korea as it is now!"

The band leaders weren't the ultimate decision makers, but I thought that might happen, and I was pretty excited. The army band in Tokyo was out. That was General Ridgeway's band and he was the commander of the Army. It was the best band of all. You had to go to Tokyo and audition for the band. Since I couldn't get off the base, there was no chance to audition. In any case, I was suddenly hopeful that I might have a chance to play music in the army after all.

The next day, I got a call over the public address system we used to call the "bitch box."

"Private Melick, report to the orderly room." Some stuff happens very slowly in the army. Other stuff happens very quickly.

Sergeant Gross was behind the desk with a yellow piece of paper. I'll never forget his name, because he was about to send me to a very different place than a Korean foxhole. Well, there's that and the fact that he had a big nameplate on his desk.

"Melick, I have your Form 20 here. Do you know what the Form 20 is?"

"No Sergeant," I replied.

"This is a record of your civilian life. Looking at this, we've decided you'd be more valuable to the United States Army in the Special Services Entertainment Division here in Japan."

I thought, I couldn't agree with you more, sergeant! But I said, "Yes sir, that would be wonderful."

He said, "Well, you'll be leaving for Yokohama tomorrow morning. Turn in your parka, turn in your rifle, and get ready to go to Yokohama."

Just that quickly, I went from the pipeline to an army bus headed for Yokohama. It seems I owed a great debt of thanks to that private in the service club. I wondered what his assignment was going to be in Korea. I sure hoped he wouldn't end up in a foxhole. It turned out all right, but I wouldn't see him again until I arrived in Hollywood in 1955. His name was Richard Long. You'll know the name if you were a fan of TV shows like *The Big Valley* or *Nanny and the Professor*. If you're too young for that, trust me, he was famous in many more circles than I was.

Yokohama, Japan

It didn't occur to me to ask Sergeant Gross what my assignment was. When he said I was headed to Yokohama, I figured I was going to be in the Yokohama Army Band because I had that good conversation with my fellow Oberlin grad—Warrant Officer Brown—on the phone.

I went out in the morning and they put me on a bus to Yokohama. I reported to the director of Special Services, not the band. My assignment was at the Yokohama R&R Center.

It seems my Form 20 gave them a different idea, and they assigned me to manage the enlisted mens' club. I would be in charge of the entertainment there for the troops coming in from the front lines on leave. There was a war on, and I was in the army, but somehow I was still going to be the piano-playing leader of the band.

The EM HUT MESS

That was the beginning of about 18 months working and living in Yokohama. I didn't have to wear my uniform except on Thursday mornings for TIP—the Troop Information Program. Everyone had to put a uniform on and go to that. At the TIP, we were told why we were in Korea—you know, besides the obvious answer that we were drafted. The rest of the time I was, for all intents and purposes, a civilian. I wore civilian clothes. I was in charge of the entertainment at the enlisted men's club—the EM HUT MESS—at the Yokohama R&R Center. I also had a desk at the Special Services headquarters.

The soldiers were on duty in Korea—most of it in combat—for six months. For every six months of fighting, they got a week off. That doesn't sound like a good deal to me, but while I was in Yokohama, it was my mission to provide the best entertainment I could. They had the choice of several places they could go and we were one of them. I'd get letters once in awhile from my buddies in Korea. As far as I know, they all lived through it. I felt bad for a while, but they never seemed to resent it. They felt good for me when they heard that I was pulled out of the pipeline. When my army stint was over, I went home for a short time and during that visit, I called a guy named McConnell, who lived fairly near me and who had trained with me and then gone to Korea. I asked him about our buddies from Basic Training and he said they had all gone to Korea together. To his knowledge, they all survived the war and were discharged and were home. This was really wonderful news.

Music: The International Language

The Korean War was a United Nations effort so I was playing for guys from all over the world, and booking entertainment. I was playing for Greeks, Turks, Australians, New Zealanders, English, Canadians, and so on. So I had to appeal to more than just Americans. It was great.

I'll never forget one time I was playing piano in the club, and these two big Ethiopian guys—they had to be at least 6'-5" —came strolling across the floor toward the piano. I'm playing something—I don't remember—and I looked up and saw these guys coming and thought, boy, I hope they're not unhappy with the music! They stopped at the piano and one of them asks, "Do you know how to play 'St. Louis Blues'?"

"Yes of course!" I said, and I started right into it.

Music is an international language. They know "St. Louis Blues" even in Ethiopia!

The Jack Melick Show

My best memories from that time are the shows that I did with the Japanese entertainers. I got to know a lot of them—the dancers, the singers, the bands, the musicians—because I would book them to come play at the EM HUT MESS. There was a terrific community of big band musicians in Japan, and they were really quite good. American music was quite popular there at that time.

I grew to love it there. I learned the language and met a lot of great musicians. Some of them became well known in the jazz field internationally later on. But when I booked them at the EM HUT mess or played with them around Japan, they were just starting.

In our "spare time," we formed the Jack Melick Show. I had a Japanese singer, a couple of Japanese tap dancers and a friend who I met there in the army; a standup comedian named Jim MacGeorge. We took 10-day leaves and the Jack Melick Show toured all over Japan.

We would go out to play at Tachikawa Air Force base and do three shows a night. We'd do a show at the Enlisted Men's Club, then the NCO Club, and the last one would be at the Officers' Club. Then the bus would always take us back to Yokohama.

You know, sometimes it was hard to realize that we were just a couple a couple hours by plane from the fighting. We played at a lot of the air bases. Those pilots had been in the air over Korea that day fighting North Korean jets. They came back, shaved and showered, had dinner, and came dancing at the Officers' Club. Looking at those guys out there, I knew they had been flying that day in combat, and were going right back out there tomorrow. You know, sometimes one of them wouldn't be there the next night. I didn't have to ask. Gave me a lot to think about.

Watching Japan Develop

It was an extraordinary time to be in Japan. It all had to do with watching post-World War II Japan develop. In the early 50's Japan was still under occupation, but recovery was underway. Certainly relations between the United States and Japan were better. I think most Americans today don't realize that the peace treaty with Japan, officially ending World War II, wasn't signed until late in 1951 and actually didn't take effect until April of 1952. And we were there, stationed in Japan as a staging point for our conflict in Korea.

All of a sudden there were symbolic and substantive changes. Almost overnight it seemed, Japan was fully Japanese again. All the army cars that we were driving around were painted black. They were no longer the wartime khaki color. The army, of course, would stay in Japan, but were no longer as visible.

We began to give back the property that we had appropriated when the war was over to the original owners. The grand movie theater in Tokyo had been called the Ernie Pyle Theater, named after the famous war journalist, but it was returned to the original owners and renamed the Toho Theater.

When I was first in Special Services in Yokohama, I didn't actually live at the Yokohama R&R Center. Those barracks were all for the guys on leave. I actually lived in the locker room area of the local baseball stadium.

When the peace treaty was signed, the stadium was also given back to the original owners. So we moved on to a small U.S. military base. I got myself a job as a night fireguard in the army theater, so I wouldn't have to sleep in the barracks. When I was there, I slept in the theater. I was supposed to be there all the time, but a lot of the time I was in Tokyo with a Japanese singer I had fallen for named Myoshi Umeki. She went by "Nancy," and she was actually well known in Japan. She was singing on radio and recording. She came to Yokohama a couple days a week with the Blue Coats Band. They wore, as you might guess, blue coats as their band uniforms. It was a BIG big band—17 or 18 pieces. They played American swing and she was the singer.

Anyway, I would take the train back down to the Yokohama station early in the morning and I'd have my motor bike locked there somewhere. I bought a little red motor bike—I guess in the U.S. we'd call it a moped. In Japan, they were called a "rabbito." I'd ride my rabbito to the EM HUT MESS in Yokohama and go to work.

In theory, I was the fireguard in our GI movie theater. I had a bedroom up there, but a lot of the time I was not there. Don't know what I would have done if there was an actual fire. Now it can be told!

Home and Back Again

My time in the army was up in the summer of 1953.

The army gave me an honorable discharge and I went home. I don't know how to explain it, but my heart remained in Japan.

I went back to Point Pleasant Beach and started playing in The Club again. But I kept thinking about Japan, and my life over there. It took about 3 months. I told my mother in the fall one day that I was going back to Japan. She said, "All right, but you have to buy your own ticket."

When I returned to Japan, I planned on resuming my relationship with Nancy Umeki. She had written to me while I was home just that short time. She sent some new pictures and wrote, "I miss you. I don't have anybody to fight with." I guess she didn't think I was coming back though, because when I got there, she had another boyfriend.

Oh well, I had another wonderful year there anyway. I used to send my folks a postcard every once in awhile, "I was at a temple in Hong Kong today. Thanks for making me practice or I wouldn't have been able to do all this."

A Year in Japan

I tooled all over Yokohama and Tokyo that year in my rabbito. I can't remember what I did with it. I sold it to somebody for $50 probably. You know, I've been telling this story for years and it's really the first time I had people say I needed to write a memoir. I'd start telling them about riding a little red motorbike around Tokyo in my tuxedo, and getting off to play in some club.

I was doing a piano act. I didn't carry a band with me. I would play, sing some ditties, get serious and then do something light again. I billed myself as a poor man's Liberace or Victor Borge. Actually, I like the Victor Borge comparison because he was a comedian too. In fact, if he wasn't a brilliant musician, he could have been a stand-up comedian. Anyway, sometimes I think I'm pretty funny and can also play the piano.

When I was looking for an apartment to rent, I told my rental agent that I needed one with a piano so I could practice. Somehow, I didn't think that was an unreasonable request in post-war Japan, but she finally found an apartment with a piano in it! It was in Nakameguro along the river in Tokyo. The owners had a bedroom that was kind of on the front slightly detached from the rest of the house. They were renting to foreigners or anybody who wanted it. The piano was in the house where the Japanese family lived.

So I moved into this room, but I found out they didn't have a telephone in the house. Well I never thought to ask. How was I going to get my bookings and keep working? It turns out there was a phone across the alley. The neighbors there had one. This family would go across the alley and use their neighbor's telephone. They told the neighbors that I would be receiving calls at that number. I gave the club managers and agents around Japan that phone number. And so I would get calls in the middle of the night sometimes.

I stayed there all that winter. It would be cold and muddy in the alley, and the neighbors from across the way would come over and knock on my door.

"Jack-san... o dingwa!" You see, "dingwa" is telephone.

"O dingwa, Jack-san."

So I'd get out of bed, put some slippers on and walk through the snow and mud to the neighbor's. But of course, you know the Japanese custom—take off your shoes before you go into someone's house. So I would wait in the hallway. They had the phone on a long extension. They'd bring the phone out to me and I'd talk on the phone. Then I'd go back across the alley. That was an adventure. That would happen several times a day really, and that was my home for the whole time I was there.

A great memory from that time was my gig as the opening act for the country star Little Jimmy Dickens. I remember that mostly because he would drink a full glass of Seagram's Seven as if it was a glass of water, and then go out and do his show! We toured Okinawa together.

If you're a little older, you might remember Little Jimmy Dickens for country songs like "Take an Old Cold Tater and Wait," "A-Sleeping at the Foot of the Bed," and "May the Bird of Paradise Fly Up Your Nose." It was fun to travel with him through Okinawa doing about a week of shows.

Back home in Tokyo, there was a bar downtown off the Ginza called Club Manuela. That was my hangout every night after I finished doing my shows wherever I was performing. I arranged for myself to play at that club. That lasted for about a week. I thought I'd be there longer, but the crowd didn't come in. It was a Japanese audience and they didn't know me that well. But you know, that didn't bother me. It was a wonderful life for a guy that wanted to play the piano and have money in his pocket.

Time to Go Home

In November 1954, I had been back in Japan for just about a year. I can't remember for sure, but I just started to get the feeling that pretty soon I'm going to have to go back home and start making a living. As much as I loved it there, I couldn't stay in the Far East forever.

Of course, I was in regular touch with my parents. They never asked me to come home, never asked when I was coming home. They always gave me my space to make decisions on my own.

I was almost 25 now, and suddenly I started to think about where my career needed to go, and while Japan would always be on my list of favorite places, it wasn't home. So... it was just time.

Jim MacGeorge

When I met Jim MacGeorge, I was standing on stage at the Club 45 NCO Club in Yokohama with a beer in my hand. I was the emcee of a floor show there, and he had just arrived in Yokohama from Fort Ord in California. A mutual friend introduced us between acts and the first thing he said was, "You shouldn't be on stage with a drink in your hand!"

I paid no attention to his obvious rudeness and asked where he was assigned. He replied, "Special Services."

I thought I was a big shot since I had been in Japan 8 or 9 months at the time so I asked him what he did in civilian life. He replied that he was a stand-up comedian and TV puppeteer. That night in Yokohama, I said I wanted to hear some of his stuff and after the show he showed me a routine he was working on. It was a takeoff on *Dragnet* he was writing and it started like this:

"Dognet! My name is Fido. I work in the Los Angeles Police Department. I'm a dog. I was home one Sunday morning, pouring over the Sunday paper..."

When I stopped laughing, we became the best of friends. We still are. That was 1952. As I write this, it's more than 60 years later.

I'm still a musician. He's still funny. We're still best friends.

Nancy Umeki

From the time we had met, I wanted to get to know her better, and one night I was talking to her, and she invited me back to Tokyo with the band. She said I could ride back with them on the band bus. Well, I wasn't in the band, to say nothing of not looking at all Japanese.

"Don't worry about it," she said.

I'm not really sure I should tell this story, but I got on the bus. Now keep in mind, I was a U.S. serviceman based at the Yokohama R&R Center. They put me down on the floor, and we went through the gate. We passed through, the guards saw a Japanese band, and away we went! They never saw me leaving the base and on we went to Tokyo.

After my visit, I caught the last train from Tokyo to Yokohama, went directly to the EM HUT MESS where our manager, Mr. Hasegawa, let me in and I sacked out in one of the R&R bunks until morning. I'd like to say that Miss Umeki invited me to stay at her apartment, but no.

From that adventure a romance developed. We dated for more than a year. Keep in mind, I was still pretty young; 21 or so. And my girlfriend was famous throughout her country. When we'd go out, people would ask for her autograph. We started to work together, and I became her accompanist when she performed. She got me on the radio, and I did several radio shows with the Blue Coats Orchestra.

Despite the typical Japanese stereotype of meekness and delicacy, she was a very strong woman, and she knew what she wanted. One time, I accompanied her at a concert in Yokohama and a reporter from a Yokohama newspaper interviewed me. I said that she was the best partner I ever had. I think I said that I was teaching her a few new songs, but mainly I said I was accompanying her. Well, when the article came out in the Yokohama newspaper, the headline read, "Army corporal finds best student in Japan." They wrote it as if I was her teacher! Somebody sent her the copy of that newspaper and she was very upset. She made it clear that she was not my student. And I couldn't agree with her more.

As I look back now, I can see that she was very driven to emigrate to the U.S. and make it there as a singer or movie star. Some time after I went home, she began dating an American agent in Japan. In fact, she did seem to gravitate to Americans in show business. She also dated another American performer in the service named Tommy Oliver. I'm not saying she was insincere when we were together, but I think she was very focused on a life and career in America.

She finally went to the United States and this agent landed her a spot on the Arthur Godfrey Talent Scouts program. She became a regular on the show. That caught the attention of a Hollywood director named Joshua Logan and he cast her in the film *Sayonara* alongside Marlon Brando and Red Buttons. She played the part of a Japanese war bride and Buttons played her husband. She became the first Asian performer ever to win an Academy Award. She and Buttons both won supporting actor Oscars that year.

She did a few more movies, but she may be most remembered for playing Mrs. Livingston (yeah, she looked like a Livingston!) on TV alongside Bill Bixby in *The Courtship of Eddie's Father*.

Al Ricketts

I learned very early in my career that it's a good idea to get to know the local newspaper Entertainment Editor or Columnist, so as soon as I felt settled in my first stay in Japan (the military one), I went to the offices of the daily *Pacific Stars and Stripes* in Tokyo. That's where I met Al Ricketts.

Corporal Ricketts was in charge of the entertainment section of the paper. In his short stint at the paper, he had become the "go-to-guy" for anybody who wanted to know about the Japanese—and particularly Tokyo/Yokohama—show biz scene. Marlon Brando, Frankie Laine, Harry James, Shirley MacLaine, and many, many others had called him, had lunch with him, or met with him when they arrived in town.

So, I went to meet him and thus began a close friendship that lasted until he died in 1969. Every time I was scheduled to play somewhere in Japan, I called him and—as if by magic—my name and show location would appear in "The Stripes." When his army stint was over, he stayed in Tokyo and became a civilian employee of the U.S. Army and continued in his same job at *The Stars and Stripes*.

When I returned to Japan as a civilian, we resumed our friendship and daily Kirin beer get-togethers. His daily column was called "On the Town with Al Ricketts." Every Sunday there would be a gathering of ex-pats from show business at his apartment with his wife Kay. The "menu" consisted of champagne and strawberries.

We also did some fun traveling together. I had met the Thai secretary of the navy on my flight back to Japan and he invited me to Bangkok. So I organized an 8-day leave and I brought Al and Don Raleigh (who was a cook and still in the service) with me. The Secretary took us around the city. It was terrific company to be with him you know.

While we were there, I took a gig for a couple nights at a resort on the Gulf of Siam. Al and Don came with me. To get there we had to take a train through the jungle. You know, it's the sort of thing you see every day... houses, countryside, steeples... and elephants. Every day? Yes!

At the resort, we met two teenage Chinese girls whose surname was Sun. It turns out that they were from the Sun Yat-Sen family. Al and I played tennis with them, and I can distinctly remember their mother sitting in the bleachers watching us play with her teenage daughters—a couple of old guys in comparison even though we were in our early 20's. I'll never forget the mother asking, "What is your rank?" And I said, "Well, I was a corporal." She wasn't asking that. She meant a rank in the diplomatic service. She thought we were diplomats because we were wearing civilian clothes. I told her we were merely traveling musicians.

That trip provided another of my biggest memories.

There was a convention of missionaries at the resort. We organized a softball game with the missionaries and we played on the beach. I was thinking while I was out there, "Here I am on the Gulf of Siam playing softball on the beach with a bunch of missionaries from America!"

The last time Al and I spent any time together was in 1968 when he and Kay were vacationing in Mazatlan, Mexico before he went to work for the Honolulu Advertiser, having left his job in Tokyo to move into civilian show business. I spent ten days there with him and Kay. He died soon after that in Hawaii at much too young an age. I think he was 41. His body just seemed to give out and he was gone.

4
A Career Begins

Time to Get Going

So it was time to move on. I had spent the last year having a lot of fun. I was working and I certainly carried my own weight financially. I had been traveling throughout Japan playing at Japanese clubs and US military installations. I probably could have kept on doing that for years. But finally I figured that I hadn't started my real career yet. I had dropped out of the American music scene for sure. So it occurred to me that if I was going to have a career in music in the United States—which of course I ultimately wanted to do—I should probably start working on it. By this time I was almost 25, so I had to get going.

Prepared for the Music Business

The Far East may not have been my final destination, but everything I did there set the stage for me. Everything I did musically for more than two years—first in the Army and then for another year on my own—contributed to my success later on. If you think about it, there wasn't a lot of pressure. I was a young American entertainer in an emerging nation that was trying to embrace everything it could of the American culture. I traveled around as an emcee of various shows. I learned how to express myself well in front of a microphone and communicate with audiences. I learned how to accompany vocalists and comedians. I learned how to write the arrangements we needed for shows. I learned how to transpose if the singer couldn't sing in the original key, and that built upon what I had started learning at Sagamore in the Poconos.

Forever grateful for my time in Japan, I think I was ready.

The Trip Home

I took my time getting back. I stopped in Hawaii and stayed there a couple days because there was a friend of mine there. His name was Johnny Uehara and he had a night club in Honolulu. He'd always have one of his waitresses take me around town while I was there. It was great to be an itinerant musician! So it was a terrific two days, and then on to my next stop in California.

Jim MacGeorge—my army buddy and the resident comedian on the Jack Melick Show—was already working in television. He got home a couple years before I did, so he had been working for two years. In late 1954, he was a voice actor on a TV show called *Time for Beany*. When I arrived in southern California, he gave me the grand tour of Hollywood. At the time, I never dreamed that I'd be back there working within a year. We took in all the sights, and he showed me everything a good tourist would want to see. I stayed there 4 or 5 days with him. So it was 6 or 7 days from Tokyo to Honolulu to Hollywood to Newark and North Plainfield.

As a side note, and I don't know why I remember this, but I brought a tape recorder home with me from Japan. They had just come out then, and it was real heavy. As we all know, Japan eventually turned into the world's electronics factory and I can say that I had one of the first tape recorders they ever made. But I carried it through the airport, out to the plane, and put it into the seat next to me. It was in a wooden case, and looked a lot like a piece of luggage. It was a Sony Type H and heavy!

The Traveling Musician

One thing that hasn't changed much over the years is the life of the traveling musician. Fortunately, I was still single and this is what I wanted to do, but being a full-time musician means that you're going to be on the road a lot of the time. I had just spent the last couple of years in the Far East, so I knew what it was like to travel. But, the United States has a whole lot more ground to cover!

Read, Fake; 24

I'd been home about a week. I put an ad in *Billboard Magazine*. In those days it was called *The Billboard*. At that time, the big band business was still pretty big. Now, *Billboard* has become way more specialized about record sales and so forth, but back then it was also about the entire music business. They had a huge classified ad section that doesn't exist today. Musicians today don't even read *Billboard*.

Anyway, everyone in the music business read it at that time. My ad read, "Read, fake; 24; sing novelty; single; union; sober; arrange, ex G.I. Excellent showman; travel anywhere." It had all the stuff that a band leader would want, I hoped!

Well, I must have received 15 telegrams and telephone calls from different band leaders or their managers the day after the magazine came out. I didn't know any of them, except for one. I had heard vaguely of a band leader named Leo Peeper. I had recently read something in *DownBeat* about him. *DownBeat* was a magazine that focused on jazz music and big bands.

They were on the road, and so I took the job with Leo Peeper at $65/week, and joined his band in Muscatine, Iowa, in November 1954.

Leo Peeper's Band

With Leo's band, I had to pay my own hotel room, which was pretty standard in the band business. He provided only transportation. I flew in to the Quad City Airport in Moline, Illinois, about 35 miles from Muscatine. I got on a bus to Muscatine and about 20 miles outside of town, I had this terrible urge to go to the bathroom. It was the toughest 20 miles I have ever ridden in my life! Finally, I got up and told the bus driver to let me off in front of the next gas station. I really didn't know where I was. I knew we were close to Muscatine, but sometimes, you know, there's just nothing you can do. When you gotta go, you gotta go!

Afterwards, I asked the attendant how far the Elk's Club was, which is where I was supposed to meet the band. Luckily, it was only six blocks away, so I walked the rest of the way and joined Leo Peeper and his big band at the Elk's Club in Muscatine, Iowa... from North Plainfield to Muscatine by way of the highway gas station.

I traveled all over the Midwest as a member of Leo's band for about 4 months. Soon after I joined the band I told him I was ready with a couple of piano specialties (I had the arrangements with me of course) if he ever wanted to feature his piano player. I wasn't trying to brag or anything, but the best big bands featured certain players—especially the piano player—as part of the show.

One of my specialties was "El Cumpanchero;" a latin number with a lot of fireworks in the right hand. The other was a boogie-woogie number. He started to feature me and raised my salary to $75 a week. Soon, he added me to the show bill—my picture there under his—and it became "Leo Peeper and His Orchestra, featuring Jack Melick."

Most of our dates were just the band at a fraternal club like an Elk's, or dance hall, or ballroom. We played one-nighters throughout Iowa, Minnesota, North Dakota—all through the midwest as far south as Oklahoma and Texas. It was called the Territory, and I'll write more on that later. There are 30 days in a month, and we'd play 28 different towns (sometimes)!

We'd stay at a hotel in Shreveport for 5 days. We'd go out to play one-nighters all around that area—Bossier City and then a town in Arkansas just a little north of there—and then come back every night to the same hotel. A country club here or there and the Petroleum Club in Shreveport. I used to pick up little souvenirs from these different places. I still have a ticket from the Petroleum Club Annual Ball in Shreveport, December 1954. "Leo Peeper and His Orchestra - $6.50 per person, dinner and dancing." What a deal!

But then there were a few special events—variety shows in which our band was one of the acts, like a state fair or auto show. I remember an auto show in Des Moines, Iowa, in December 1954. We accompanied The Four Step Brothers, a great tap dancing troupe, and Julius La Rosa, a very well-known singer who had made a name for himself on the TV variety show, *Arthur Godfrey and His Friends*.

We had a totally inexperienced drummer in the band, really a beginner as I think back now. La Rosa just didn't want to work with us because of the drummer. He quit after the first day, got on a plane, and went back to New York.

Well, we were at the auto show there on a two-week deal. There were thousands of people coming through from all over the state. They'd look at all the cars during the day, and we'd perform at night. La Rosa was the headliner. When he left, the Four Step-Brothers became the headliners, so in a sense, we did too since we were the accompanying band. Leo had me do my piano numbers in the show. It was a lot of fun and I remember a pretty good write-up in the local papers.

The booker of the band, out of Omaha, then sent a lady out to replace Julius La Rosa. Her name was Dagmar. That's it, she just went by Dagmar. She had some fame too from a New York TV show called *Broadway Open House*. She was blond, tall—maybe 5-10 or more—and big all over, if you know what I mean. If you remember the old Cadillacs of the 40's and 50's, they had these missile-pointed front bumpers. A lot of the other car manufacturers picked them up too and they were everywhere in the 50's. When she became popular, they became known as Dagmar Bumpers, for reasons I'll let you think about. Anyway, she created this comic "dumb blond" character and became the headliner.

Of all things, I can remember sitting with Norman Butler, the lead alto sax player and manager of the band, on the second level of this huge auditorium. We're looking down at the cars in Des Moines, Iowa in the winter of 1954. I said, "I wonder if I'll ever come back here and be the leader of my own band? Because that's what I want to do."

So I always remember exactly what I wanted to do, and it always seemed to me like I was headed in the right direction.

Even so, I remember a not-so-pleasant glance into the future when we played a one-nighter in St. Louis at the Casa Loma Ballroom. They told us there'd be another band there. "A group of guys are going to play there during your intermissions."

When we took a break, these five guys came out and they started playing rock and roll, and getting louder and louder. At one point, the bass man laid down on his back and put his bass up in the air. He was playing it upside down!

We looked at each other and said, "What the hell is that?"

Our band manager looked at us and replied, "That, my friends, is the future, and it doesn't look good for us!"

The name of the group was the Comets, and they were led by a guy named Bill Haley. It was just before they recorded "Rock Around the Clock."

Jimmy "Dancin' Shoes" Palmer's Band

After I'd been with Leo for about four months, I got a call from Jimmy Palmer, a band leader from Chicago. He was slightly up scale from Leo Peeper's band from Omaha. He said he'd heard about me, they were looking for a piano player, and wanted to know if I'd be interested in joining his band at $105 a week. Now this was 1955, and in 1955, $105 week for a band musician was a lot of money. So that was hard to beat, but I didn't go with him strictly because of the money.

The thing that intrigued me was the schedule they were going to play. They were playing 25–30 days a month, just like Leo's band. But they had two weeks at the Hollywood Palladium in May of 1955. Now, that caught my eye—to go out to Hollywood to play at the world-famous Hollywood Palladium for two weeks. For me, there was just one more thing. I had my piano solos and told Jimmy that I needed to be featured with him just as I had been with Leo. He said, "That's all right, I heard about those solos. I want you to do them." This became an offer I couldn't pass up.

Jimmy Palmer's nickname was "Dancin' Shoes." He had two little blocks of wood with sandpaper on them, and when we did a broadcast, he would scrape those little blocks of wood together to make a rhythmic scratching sound. His next words were, "Come on kiddies, lose your blues, let's put on those dancin' shoes." And the band would start to play. He was a character.

We worked a similar kind of schedule that Leo Peeper did around the Midwest; Fargo, Omaha, Illinois, Iowa, Minnesota. His band was very popular, more than Leo's. Ballroom dancing was still very, very popular and you could keep a band working all the time.

Another kind of side note. One time we played in Springfield, Illinois. We played at a place there called the Lake Club. We were there for two weeks, and the headliners were the Mills Brothers. So we accompanied the Mills Brothers. Well, the Mills Brothers were baseball nuts. They carried baseball equipment with them on the road! Sometime during their stay, they'd try to find a field to go to, and play baseball or softball. So on this trip, we found a field with the waiters, the waitresses, the band, and the Mills Brothers and played baseball. Years later, I saw them in Los Angeles and showed them old pictures of us playing baseball in Springfield, Illinois. You know, it didn't mean that much to them because they played baseball every place they went, but it meant a lot to me. So that was a blast with the Mills Brothers. I'll never forget it. They were great guys!

So at the end, we did a couple weeks going through west Texas, New Mexico, and Yuma, Arizona. We headed to California and played at March Air Force Base and the San Diego Naval Air Station, and then ended up in Los Angeles at the Hollywood Palladium.

The Territory

As I wrote before, starting in the late 20's and through the 30's, ballroom dancing was very, very big. The "territories" comprised numerous dance ballrooms throughout the United States, mostly in the midwest and southwest from Minnesota to Texas. And every town, even small ones, would have a ballroom or hall where there would be dancing. Even though the heyday was in the 20's and 30's, these ballrooms were going strong even into the 1960's.

The band booker would line up a schedule where the band would play in Davenport, Iowa for a one-nighter at a big ballroom called The Coliseum. Next stop was Muscatine, Iowa at the Elks Club. Then it was on to Dubuque at another Elks Club there. It was like that—doing the rounds of these halls and clubs at 200 or 300 miles every day. Jimmy's booking agent was out of MCA's Chicago office, and Leo had a smaller agency out of Omaha.

Leo Peeper and Jimmy Palmer were territory bands. Leo Peeper and his Orchestra primarily made the rounds in the midwest, but Jimmy Palmer was more popular and made his way also through the southwest to California and the east coast.

Territory bands traveled on a bus, or in caravans of cars. In Leo's case, we traveled on a bus. I loved it. Of course if you're single, healthy, 24 and doing what you love to do, riding around in a broken down school bus is not going to hurt! And Leo's bus was old. We could sleep in it if we had to, but it would break down all the time. Still, I don't recall that we ever missed a job.

Jimmy Palmer traveled in cars, with four guys to a car. He paid three or four guys to drive, and each one took two or three musicians with him. He followed in a panel truck with all the band's equipment. That's the way we went.

Making the Day Sheet

In the midwest, in particular, a certain chain of hotels catered to the traveling musicians. It was $2.50 per night with two musicians in each room.

They had a system called the "Day Sheet," and the Day Sheet was the start of the business day when the receipts and check-ins for that day started. You didn't have to check out by that hour of the morning, but if you came in early in the morning when the Day Sheet started, you could register for that day.

So we would arrive at the next town, if possible, about the time that the Day Sheet was starting. We'd ride all night in the bus, arrive at the town, and sit in the lobby of this particular hotel chain until the Day Sheet was available which was usually around 7:30 or 8:00 a.m. And when it was available, the band manager would give us the word to go register. We'd go up to our rooms and sleep a few hours. Then we'd get up, have lunch, go to an afternoon movie or whatever and go to work. After playing that night, we'd go back to the hotel and go to bed again. We'd sleep twice for that day, paying once, check out the next morning, and drive the next day to the next city.

We couldn't make the next Day Sheet because we were driving during the day. But when we'd drive overnight, we'd make the Day Sheet.

And that phrase has been unfamiliar to almost everyone I have talked to except old traveling salesmen who traveled through the midwest. They knew what the Day Sheet was. They would time it so they could sleep twice for one night's pay. You'd sleep in the morning and then come back at night and sleep again. I've often thought that if I ever wrote a book about the music business, I'd call it *Making the Day Sheet*. Of course, I found out that hardly anybody knows what the Day Sheet is, so that's not a good title.

The Audiences

The people we played for just liked to dance. Neither one of these two bands I played for were what we would call jazz bands or show bands. They were strictly dance bands. So we'd start to play and they would come out and dance. That's why they were there. We played clubs and ballrooms. And these were great people who loved this kind of music and who loved to dance.

We were in South Dakota a couple of times, and we would play on Indian reservations. So obviously, most of the people that came to the dance were Native Americans. Now most of us were from back east, so we had never seen Indians, or Native Americans, before. Of course, as young single guys, we were mostly concerned whether there were any cute Indian girls there. But they liked the music, so I remember how interesting that was. 'Nuff said.

But no matter where we went, they danced. You know, it's a different kind of music, so they didn't scream and holler like a rock crowd would, but they danced.

Two Weeks at the Palladium

At the time the Palmer band arrived in Hollywood, the Hollywood Palladium broadcast a TV show every Tuesday night called *Dance Time at the Palladium*. Whatever band was booked there during any given week had a one-hour TV show on Tuesday night. So we opened on a Monday and the second night we're on a KTLA-TV telecast. On the night of the broadcast, I did a solo in the first half-hour. During the intermission, the director of the show, came back to Jimmy.

"Mr. Landsberg likes your pianist. Is he going to do another solo?"

Jimmy answered, "Yeah, he has another solo in the second half."

"Fine, Mr. Landsburg likes him." So I played my other solo in the second half.

The next morning I got a call at the hotel, and it was from Klaus Landsberg's office at KTLA. Klaus Landsberg was one of the pioneers of live television and he was the owner and station manager at KTLA. He loved live music, and he was the one who had seen me on his show the night before. He asked if I wanted to stay in Hollywood and play on TV. And I thought, you know, this is moving pretty fast! This was only about 8 or 9 months since I got back from Japan, and I was already in Hollywood with the offer of a TV job.

I said, "Yeah, I would love to."

He said, "Well, come on down to the station. We want to meet you in person."

I went down to the studio. KTLA was in Charlie Chaplin's old studio on Sunset Boulevard. Klaus liked me a lot and I certainly liked him.

You know, there was nothing I could do but say "yes."

Lessons from the Road

My territory band experience wasn't all that long, but I learned more things about leading a band—what to do and what not to do. I learned more about talking to the musicians during the performance and during rehearsals.

And I was thinking about my having my own band the whole time. The plan was going right. It wasn't exactly an organized plan, but I had always committed myself to go anywhere I needed to go. I was still single, so I could go. I never thought that I had to get off the road and teach, or start a family. I never said, "I better get off the road like a lot of guys do." I always kept going because that's what I wanted to do.

And now I was in Hollywood.

Leo Peeper

I'll never forget when I made the decision to leave Leo and join Jimmy Palmer's band. We were playing at the Aragon Ballroom in Chicago at the time and I went up to see Leo and give him the news. He was staying at the old Croydon Hotel. He was real sick. He could hardly talk. I really felt bad about it because he was a very nice guy. And he had just printed about 150 8" x 10" glossies of me at the piano, "featured with Leo Peeper and His Orchestra."

To top it all off, he didn't like Jimmy Palmer!

So I said, "Look Leo, I was offered this job with Jimmy Palmer and I think I ought to take it because they're going to go to Hollywood."

He said, "Well, Jimmy's not much of a nice guy."

"Well, it's gonna be all right," I said, "and the pay is a little bit better, but that's not the main reason. The main reason is he's got two weeks coming up in Hollywood."

"Ok," Leo said, "there's really nothing I can do about it, sick or not."

Our relationship was very good. Although I would say I learned the most from Orrin Tucker later about how to be a band leader, I owe a big debt to Leo. It was from him I learned how to play a waltz. It was years later and he had retired in Dallas. I was playing at a dance hotel in Ft. Worth and Leo was with his wife. The band was playing the "Anniversary Waltz" and he got up from the table and came up to me and said, "Well, I see you still know how to play a waltz!" You see, I was playing it the way he had taught me 30 years earlier.

That was nice. I will always remember him being my first boss and a nice guy.

Jimmy Palmer

I didn't feel quite the same way about Jimmy Palmer. He was okay. He was never mean, but I felt closer to Leo.

Jimmy featured me and had me do at least two solos every night. Unlike Leo, he was very upset when I quit. I told him that Klaus Landsberg had offered me a contract with KTLA and I had to take it.

He said he didn't think I should. He said that he was giving me a chance to get out of there—to get out of Hollywood. I'm thinking, wait a minute, I just got here.

I said, "But I like it here."

He said he wanted two weeks notice anyway, and I agreed to that. In the meantime, he called the *Daily Variety* and told them that the head of KTLA was tampering with his musicians and raiding his band. In the end, he got several days of good publicity out of it. The *Daily Variety* came and interviewed me, Mr. Landsberg, and publicized the whole thing.

So, I went back out on the road with Jimmy. I didn't play my two solos anymore. We ended up in Fargo, North Dakota when the two weeks was up, and he drove me to the airport, wished me well, and said, "I don't think you're going to make it there."

"Maybe not," I said, "but I really have to give it a try, Jimmy." So he told me that if anything went wrong to call him. I got on the plane, and never saw him again.

But he was trying to tell me that it was going to be tough out there. I don't think he was trying to be nasty or anything. I was just 24 or 25 at the time. I guess in his eyes, guys my age weren't supposed to land great jobs in Hollywood!

Well, turns out he was wrong. It wasn't really that tough. I've stayed in the dance band business for more than 60 years. Now, I never became a nationwide name, never famous (except in certain circles, of course). But I still made it, because I never was out of work and I continually got hired.

About four months or so after I left Jimmy Palmer, one of his band member's cars was involved in a serious highway accident on the way to Norfolk, Nebraska, to play at the Kings Ballroom. A total of 10 people were killed, four of them in Jimmy's band. It was horrible. I knew these guys.

5
Hollywood!

Landing in Hollywood

So there I was—25 years old and a steady job in Hollywood. I moved out of the hotel and into a very nifty downtown apartment on Cahuenga Boulevard. There were entertainment people all around it right in the middle of Hollywood. It was a great place for a single musician to live. I was just taking in everything that was there.

The Palladium turned out to be a turning point.

KTLA-TV had this relationship with the Palladium broadcasting *Dance Time at the Palladium* from there on Tuesday nights. I didn't know this at the time, but they had plans together. Sterling Way, who owned the Palladium at the time, and Klaus Landsberg agreed that the band Landsberg put on KTLA would also play regularly at the Palladium.

So while I was there, mainly doing the TV show, we played month-long engagements at the world-famous Palladium. Tommy Dorsey played there when they opened it. Four thousand people were there on his opening night. To play at the Hollywood Palladium... there was nothing else like it at the time.

It ought to be a monument. It opened in 1940 and Dorsey had a young guy named Frank Sinatra singing with him at the time. I don't remember what became of him. The Palladium is still going. It has the advantage of being a real concert hall, so even though big band music has faded away, the Palladium itself has not.

Getting my Card

I didn't have a union card to play in Hollywood. I had one from Ohio from my days at Oberlin, but at that time, the Hollywood musician's union had a rule that a guy from another town couldn't start on a steady job immediately. They were just trying to protect the local guys. A new musician had to come in and do one-nighters, or anything he could, to establish himself. And at the end of three months, he could apply for membership in the local.

Well, KTLA couldn't wait three months. This TV show was coming right up. So Klaus Landsberg, Sterling Way, and I went to the union in Hollywood. We went into the president's office and these two men said, "We need this guy now," or something to that effect.

These were two big employers and they used a lot of musicians. KTLA had about 5 or 6 live band shows at the time. One was called *Frosty Frolics* and came from an ice skating rink in Garden Grove. Another was a country and western dance show called *Western Follies*. There was another called *Bandstand Review* on Sunday nights. Lots of live music. At the same time, big bands played at the Palladium 52 weeks a year.

So when owners like these two said, "we need this guy—" the union was more than willing to cooperate. The local president—and I forget his name now—called the secretary in and said, "Give Mr. Melick a card."

The Orrin Tucker Show

KTLA had another live music show every Friday night. It was a local show, of course, and was becoming very popular in southern California as far as channel 5 reached; from Bakersfield in the north all the way down to San Diego. Every Friday night at 8:00pm, southern Californians tuned in to *The Lawrence Welk Show*.

The Lawrence Welk Show was so popular in southern California that ABC television—which KTLA was not affiliated with—offered Welk a spot on their coast-to-coast network on Saturday nights. So you really couldn't blame Welk for moving on. But Klaus Landsberg, president of KTLA, loved live music, and he didn't want to lose the audience that Welk's show had brought to KTLA. So he decided to put on another music show Friday nights in that popular 8:00 o'clock hour with another band leader.

The band leader he hired was Orrin Tucker—the famous band leader I had been enthralled with at the Strand Theater in New York when I was only 11. Orrin was a very personable guy, a good showman, and Mr. Landsberg thought that he would be a good man to do this show in place of Welk.

Welk always had featured players in his show. So, Mr. Landsberg told Orrin that he wanted to do the same thing with this show. He wanted Orrin to bring his band, but then Mr. Landsberg added five or six featured musicians to play in the band and do solos on the show. I was fortunate enough to be one of them.

Now you have to understand it would be very unusual in the music business for an employer or booking agent to tell a band leader who to have in his band, especially the featured players.

In fact, it just wasn't done. But this wasn't your run-of-the-mill TV station, and Klaus Landsberg wasn't in the music business! This was show business. Orrin agreed because this was his opportunity to get his band on television. The band was led by Orrin Tucker, featuring Bobby Bruce on violin, Ernie Ball on guitar, and Jack Melick on piano, among others. Elmer Schmidt was featured on the vibraphone, and Landsberg liked the "crystal sound" of that instrument. So he named the band the "Crystal Tone Orchestra." So we were all members of Orrin Tucker's Crystal Tone Orchestra whether he liked it or not!

It turned out that Orrin was very gracious about it. He was a real gentleman. I'll never know exactly how he felt about it, but I know that if it was me, I would not have liked it! And maybe he didn't either, but he never let on one way or the other. (Incidentally, he lived to be 100. He died not too long ago in 2011. He took a personal liking to me, and he and I remained friends until he died.)

So that's what happened. He kept his regular pianist, a real nice guy named Billy Rose, and I played second piano during ensemble numbers. When I had my solos, they would roll another piano out front for me. I did two solos every Friday night. My salary at KTLA was $110 per week, and then I got a $25 a week raise every six months. I signed a two-year contract, so I was close to $200 a week when the contract ended. This was 1955 and 1956, so I was flush! Klaus Landsberg, Orrin Tucker, and the Crystal Tone Orchestra were very, very good to me.

On Fridays, we would go in about 10:00 in the morning and rehearse until about 4:00 or 4:30. We'd have a lunch break in there, and take a dinner break after we finished. We came back dressed in our tuxedos, and the show went on at

8:00 p.m. It was emceed by Orrin Tucker as the band leader. We were very similar to the Lawrence Welk show in style, playing the same type of good, commercial dance music. The featured players would perform solos during the show. It was a nice stage setup, with a studio audience and it was a big audience. Lots of people watched us on television at first. Just as Mr. Landsberg predicted, we kept the Lawrence Welk audience, at least for awhile. Fortunately for us, Welk's show was on Saturday night, so it was not in direct competition.

There was a singer on our show named Roberta Linn. Roberta was one of Lawrence Welk's first "Champagne Ladies." She had left the show before Welk went to ABC, and I think Mr. Landsberg believed she was another addition that would make the show a success. She left after about a year, and then there was a turnover of other singers. Harry Babbitt joined us for awhile. Harry had been the featured vocalist with Kay Kyser's band. Orrin himself also sang and played the saxophone. Joanie O'Brien—who also did movies and TV—sang with us and she was very popular too.

But we also had some pretty good musicians. Our featured guitar player was Ernie Ball. When the show went off the air, he went into the guitar business and has become one of the biggest names in that industry. If you want to buy guitar strings, picks, or guitars, Ernie Ball is the name of the company to get them from, even today. He became a very big part of the guitar industry.

Our drummer was Dave Alpert. You may know the name because his brother was Herb Alpert, founder of the Tijuana Brass. Dave and I became very good friends because we were about the same age and had been in the Korean War at the same time.

When I started to form my own little groups, the trios and stuff around town, Dave was my drummer for a lot of that. Dave, Herb, and a fellow named Bob Moss formed a record label called A&M Records and were probably one of the biggest labels in the 60's and 70's.

Fan Mail

We all got fan mail. I'd been in the music business for at least a few years now, but I had never gotten fan mail. You know, when you were on the road, the people got to see you one time, and they didn't take the time to write you a letter. But television was different. They got to see us every week.

And I got a letter every week from a lady in San Diego who critiqued my performances. I'm not sure her critiques were educated, but I saved her first letter because it was the first "fan letter" I ever got!

Then I used to get sort of a love letter from a girl that lived around Los Angeles somewhere. How she just fell in love watching my hands on the piano, I'll never know. Finally, after about 6 or 8 months of that, she sent me a picture of herself in her underwear. I never met her, but that's my one and only obsessed fan story!

The Leader of the Band

I watched Orrin very carefully every night as I watched the band leader very carefully with every band I was with. Sometimes when I was on the road with Jimmy Palmer, he would go all night without talking to the audience. I always thought that even if you're in a bad mood or don't feel well, you have to put that aside. I thought that when I have my own band, no matter how I feel, I'm not going to go through a whole evening without communicating with the people. Communicating with the audience is absolutely important. Orrin was that kind of leader.

As the leader, you look at them and smile at them and talk to them during the breaks. You find out what they want and you remember their names. You sit down at their table if they invite you to do so during intermissions. You don't disappear into the band room.

Some leaders were so good at communicating that they become well known just by their personality and their appearance as a front man, and not necessarily through their musical ability. Kay Kyser was one of those. So were Horace Heidt and Sammy Kaye. They were not really great musicians, but they could communicate with their audience. The audience had a good time and enjoyed themselves that night. They went home thinking, "Gee, we had a great time. When that band comes back to town, let's go again."

Orrin was all of that, and he was a good musician, too.

I'm good as the leader. I know also that, as a pianist, there are plenty of guys who fundamentally play the piano better than I do. But no one's had the longevity that I've had. I do feel that I know more about playing good dance music than anybody, anywhere. And that's our success really because we play, I think, terrific dance music. I don't think there's a better dance band in the country or a better leader. Of course, I can say that now since there's not that many of us left!

Back in those KTLA days, I also learned some

fundamental things that surprise me today. I mean "surprise" because I was so dumb not to know them then. For example, I took an arrangement of "Near You" and made it into a piano solo for me. I wrote some band parts for the orchestra to play. So I circled the parts that the instruments were to play, and didn't circle the parts I didn't want them to play. When we went into the rehearsal they did just the opposite. They came in when the parts weren't circled and laid out during the circled parts.

Bobby Bruce, the lead violinist, said, "Well Jack, the things that you circled are what we don't play."

I said, "Oh, I circled where I want you to play." That seemed logical to me.

He said, "No, you circle the parts we don't play."

That was one basic thing I didn't even know. I didn't study arranging. I just taught myself from my regular musical knowledge. You know, I had to write parts for different instruments, but it never occurred to me that when you're in a rehearsal, you circle the parts you don't want them to play. I learned many of the fundamental things, playing with these terrific Hollywood musicians.

The Keys

The Orrin Tucker Show was only one night a week, of course. We rehearsed all day Friday and the show was Friday night. So I took a job playing the piano in a place called The Keys, which was across the street from Universal Studios. The bar was called The Keys, not only because there was a piano in there, but the owner was a guy named Eddie Keys. What a perfect combination!

Eddie was also an employee at Universal. He saved his money and opened a bar right across the street. Eddie Keys became a good friend and I played there until I left Hollywood many years later.

I played there on Friday and Saturday nights. I'd get there about 9:30 on Friday after the TV show, and then play Saturday all evening on a regular schedule. The place was populated with the people who worked at Universal Studios, including some movie names you might have heard of. At that time, the "studio system" was in place, and these young actors would sign 7-year contracts. The studio would hope to make them stars, and they essentially "belonged" to Universal. They could only work for that particular studio for the 7 years of their contract.

They all came over to The Keys during breaks and after work. One of the first I saw was Richard Long, the young private who got me out of the pipeline in Korea. We re-established our friendship and I got to know his wife, Mara Corday. We'd talk about Camp Drake in Tokyo. Quite often, I'd be sitting with him and someone would sit down and I'd say, "This is the man that saved my life in the Far East."

That'd make him mad and he'd say, "Will you stop telling people I saved your life?"

"Well Dick," I'd say, "I was on my way to Korea and you called Tokyo and Yokohama to get me a job in Japan. So quite possibly you saved my life. At the very least, you saved me from freezing in a parka with an M-1 all winter!" But anyway, he didn't want to take credit for saving my life.

Bill Reynolds was another guy I had met in Japan. He was a classical music disc jockey and announcer on U.S.

Armed Forces Radio. By the time I got to Hollywood, Bill Reynolds was a young actor and his biggest success was later on *The FBI* on Sunday nights. Efrem Zimbalist, Jr. was the star and Bill played Zimbalist's younger partner. So he had 5 years of coast-to-coast TV at that time. In 1956 he made a movie called *Away All Boats*. There was a theme song of the same name. The composer of that tune—Frank Skinner—came into The Keys one night and asked me if I would play "Away All Boats" on the TV show sometime. Well, that was a huge compliment too. He was a very well known composer and arranger. So he came in, asked me to write an arrangement of "Away All Boats," and play it on our show, which was really an honor. I was glad to do it.

I also met Clint Eastwood, David Janssen, and a young guy named David Andrews and his father Dana; already a famous movie actor who also hung out at The Keys. It was the whole Universal crew, including camera people, makeup people, lighting people, electric people, and stunt men. There's one well-known stunt man I remember named Bobby Hoy. The studio was right across the street.

I also met my first wife there. It wasn't a real good marriage. She was Rock Hudson's secretary at that time. Eventually she got a few roles on TV and movies herself. We had a son who is still working on a career in Hollywood as an assistant director. He's John T. Melick, III.

John's mom later married an actor named John Aniston. They had a daughter who went on to a Hollywood career as well. I met my son's half-sister for the first time when I went to visit him. This very young little girl asked me, "Are you my brother's daddy?" I told her that I was.

John and I talk to each other by phone these days and I get to see him and his family when I venture out to California. I even get to talk to my son's half-sister once in a blue moon as well, but not very often. She's pretty busy most days. Unlike her "brother's daddy," Jennifer Aniston is famous in more than just certain circles.

Anyway, some of my patrons liked to critique my solo number when I arrived after the TV show. They usually got there well before I did and they would have watched it there at The Keys from 8 to 9. They would stop the jukebox and actually watch the show. So when I came in the door at 9:30 or so, they'd critique what they thought about it. They'd have a real good time with it.

"You looked at the camera too much!"

"Get that stupid Liberace smile off your face!"

Real professional critics. This went on every Friday, and I stayed at The Keys even after the Orrin Tucker show went off the air.

Many of the regulars became stars, and these were the ones that I got to know. They were all regular people. It wasn't the big egos you hear about today. Well, maybe a little... after Janssen got a little bit famous, he got kind of, you might say, self-important. After awhile, he'd see me and he'd say, "Hey Melick! Yokohama!" He'd yell at me across the room, and that would be it. We didn't talk much. He just remembered that I had been in Yokohama with Jim MacGeorge.

The Hollywood Scene

I lived right in Hollywood for the first six months or so after I start working at KTLA. I wanted to absorb the Hollywood scene. I went to the Brown Derby, and I went to the Palladium when we weren't working there. I could get in the back door and I'd bring a girl with me and dance to Les Brown's band all night. Everybody knew me there.

If I got a little overweight, I'd go to Norm's Coffee Shop on Sunset Boulevard and get a thin steak sandwich with sliced tomatoes instead of a big juicy steak and french fries. I'd get this steak sandwich with black coffee or iced tea every day and lose a couple of pounds. Or I was having lunch at Nicodell Restaurant in downtown Hollywood, seeing who was around and listening to the biggest lies about what their next show was going to be about.

So I worked all week writing music or listening to great live music—Kenton's band, Woody Herman's band, and the Mills Brothers. Just about everybody played there because it was Hollywood you know. But finally, to tell the truth, I got sick of that Hollywood phoniness because everybody was just talking about themselves and what they were going to do next. I got tired of that after a few years. That part I don't miss.

I made friends with a guy named Jimmy Itagaki, a Japanese American who owned a restaurant in L.A.'s downtown "Little Tokyo." I'd go there late at night almost every night. I'd get down there about midnight and drink Sake with the Japanese staff and the Japanese musicians. I still had that feeling about Japan and had loved it so much over there.

I purposely tried to speak as much Japanese as possible. I wasn't really fluent. I couldn't talk about world affairs, you know, but I got around everywhere in Japan speaking basic Japanese. So I practiced it every chance I got. The Japanese people always appreciated when you made the effort to speak their language. I also learned some Japanese songs to play.

Jim MacGeorge was already in Hollywood. He had become successful as a voice actor in a cartoon show that was nationally famous called *Beany and Cecil*. He was making good money for that time, and he and I resumed our friendship. It was quite a coincidence to be buddies over in Yokohama in Special Services and then together again in Hollywood. I'm on Channel 5 and he's on Channel 11 and we're hanging out in Hollywood together.

We double dated a lot. We went to Big Bear and Lake Arrowhead. He had a girlfriend named Gloria and later on another one named Helen. I dated a couple of girls whose names I can't even remember now! But we were gentlemen. We'd do overnight stays and the girls would be in one room and we'd be in another. We'd go out to Santa Monica or Malibu to a nice seafood restaurant on the water with our girlfriends.

The End of the Show

The ratings for the *Orrin Tucker Show* continued to go down. In the end, we didn't keep very many of the Lawrence Welk fans. He had a style all his own, and you couldn't replace that with Orrin Tucker nor anybody else for that matter. So after about a year and a half, the show went off the air. I had a semi-annual renewable contract with Channel 5. I had just entered my fourth six-month period at the time the show folded, so they kept me on to the end. I played guest shots with some of the other musical programs they had on the air at the time.

One was *Western Varieties*. The leader of that was a well-known western band leader named Doye O'Dell. Another on Sunday nights was called *Bandstand Review*. The band leader's name there was Leighton Noble. They played the top ten hit parade songs of the week. I also continued playing at the Keys.

Well, as things were about to wrap up at KTLA, my good fortune and perfect timing continued. An agent from MCA, Inc., Bob Willding, called me and asked if I would like to sign with MCA. At the time, MCA had the largest talent agency in the United States. MCA was founded in the 20's and had its hand in almost every aspect of the entertainment business from music to talent to movies. It doesn't exist any more as a talent agency, but its various businesses have all been absorbed by other well-known companies. Anyway, Bob asked me if I had any desire to be a band leader myself.

I said, "Yes, that's what I always wanted to be."

He replied, " Well, we've been watching you on Orrin's show, and we think that you'd be a great band leader."

And that's when I officially became the Leader of the Band!

Orrin Tucker

I learned a lot about being a band leader from Orrin Tucker.

He had a unique way of treating his band members. When rehearsing my bands before I met Orrin—in fact most band leaders do it this way—I would say, for instance, "At letter A, we want that to be louder. So saxes play a little bit louder. Trumpets, we want that to be short..." You know, it was in sort of a commanding way.

Orrin, on the other hand, would say, "How would it be if the saxes played a little bit louder at letter A?"

He didn't stand up there and say, "You saxes really screwed up that part. I want the saxes to play louder at A." He didn't command, he suggested. "How would it be...?"

Then we'd play it and he'd say, "That's what I want. That's good." I never forgot that.

Orrin also taught me how to start every set for dancing. He said, "When you're playing a tune for dancing, don't have a long introduction where there's no beat. They'll walk off the floor by the time you get into the rhythm, and the dance floor's empty."

I had a song I liked to do in my solos. It was "Autumn Leaves," which starts with a big drum roll and brass, and it's not really in a dance tempo. So the way I had it, the drums are rolling and I'm pounding on the piano, and the people on the dance floor are waiting for the dance beat to begin.

He'd tell me, "Even though they're dramatic on the recordings, when you're in the dance hall, you'll see that people walk off the floor. They don't know if you're going to play a rumba, a jitterbug, or what." So I remembered that and never wrote any more long introductions.

I thought he was a terrific leader. He was Klaus Landsberg's pick for that job on Channel 5 because he had a nice personality, and he loved to communicate with the audience. I watched him do that. I got a lot of that from him. One of my big things is that I communicate with the audience, and they like that. He was such a good guy, and he took a personal liking to me.

Klaus Landsberg

He passed away too young. Died of cancer when he was just 40 years old. He was a German-born television pioneer and the general manager of KTLA. They called him "Mr. Television" at the station. He came to the United States in the late 30's and eventually organized the then-Paramount station in Los Angeles; Channel 5, KTLA.

Best of all, he was a fan of the music. He developed all the great music shows on KTLA; *Frosty Frolics, Bandstand Review, Western Varieties, Dixie Showboat, The Lawrence Welk Show*, and of course, *The Orrin Tucker Show* featuring the Crystal Tone Orchestra.

If Klaus Landsberg had not been directing *Dance Time at the Palladium* that night in April 1955, and had not asked for another solo number from the pianist... well... let's just say that three-fourths of this book would never have happened!

My beloved grandfather, William J. (Pop) Stryker, and me, at 6 years of age, are performing a duet in the Melick family parlor in 1936. (JACK MELICK)

Pop Stryker with me and my younger sister Jane, circa 1938. (JACK MELICK)

John T. Melick, Jr. at age 10 in 1938. Since I had already announced my intention to be a big band leader at the age of 6, I'm a wily veteran of 4 years by this point. (LORSTAN STUDIOS)

The band director (left) at North Plainfield High School in the absence of Maestro Joe Schaedel, fall 1946. About 20 years later (right), the maestro pays me a visit in Dallas. (JACK MELICK)

My first band while still in high school, the Jack Melick Orchestra, in 1946. Billy, Natalie, Johnny, Dickie, Tony, Lou, Herby, Charlie, and Jack. (JACK MELICK)

Camp Sagamore in Milford, Pennsylvania. Not a bad way to spend the summers, entertaining with my band (and bell-hopping luggage to the guests' rooms) from 1946-1948. (JACK MELICK)

Mom and Dad came to visit me often those summers in Sagamore. This is them in 1946. (JACK MELICK)

My Oberlin College band in 1949; Lee, Claire, Tommy, Eddie, Pappy, Seymour, Al, Rollo, Ann, and Jack (striking my version of Stan Kenton's signature pose). (JACK MELICK)

With my idol, the great Stan Kenton, circa 1953. (BROOKS EDLER)

Private Jack Melick performing with local musicians at the Yokohama R&R Center, circa 1952. (JACK MELICK)

Performing with Myoshi (Nancy) Umeki in 1952 while stationed in Japan. (JACK MELICK)

NOVEMBER 6, 1954 THE BILLBOARD MERCHANDISE 71

MUSICIANS

A-1 SINGING PIANIST—SOPHISTICATED material; doubles organ, accordion; interested Florida engagement. Available December 15. Photos. Bobby Barnes, c/o Billboard, New York 36. no6

ALTO SAX-CLARINET—AGE 37; SINGLE, sober; commercial experience. Desires connection with same. Robert Sitler, Granby, Mo.

EXPERIENCED LADY PIANIST-SOLOVOX solo, orchestra; read, fake, transpose; accompanist. Dramatic and radio experience. Gladys Bell, Marquette Hotel, Denver, Colo.

GIRL BASS PLAYER FOR COMBO OR full band; read, fake, sober, single; union; 24; willing to travel, arrange, experienced. Jean McIninich, Brownville, Neb.

GUITAR—ELECTRIC LEAD OR RHYTHM; read or fake. Popular style; good voice; well experienced. Write. Florida or vicinity only. Alfred Bronson, General Delivery, Coral Gables, Fla. no27

GUITAR—MODERN LEAD AND RHYTHM; vocals, solo or parts. Five years top trio. G. Erickson, Harmon Hotel, Minneapolis, Minn.

BASSMAN—READ, FAKE, SOME VOCALS. O. Woolsey, 1118 First St., Chillicothe, Mo. Phone 2330W.

LEAD TENORMAN—CLARINET, Bb BASS sax, desires location, night club job; name band experience; read, fake, go, cut show, arrange, group sing. Sober, neat appearance, dependable, married. Snapshot on request. Can join immediately. Nighter, lay off. Al Gaffney, 510 First St., N.E., Mandan, N. D. no13

PIANIST FOR COMMERCIAL BIG BAND—Read, fake; 24; sing novelty; single; union; sober; arrange, ex G.I. Excellent showman; travel anywhere. Jack Melick, 188 Belmont, North Plainfield, N. J.

RECORDING Bb BASS HORN—READ and fake; age 27; exp. all lines. Lonnie Harris, 2017 Pacific Ave., Venice, Calif.

SAX, TENOR OR ALTO — DOUBLING clarinet and flute. Lead or jazz chair. Conservatory graduate, arranger, name experience. Musician, 625 Garfield St., Middletown, Ohio.

My classified ad that first appeared in the November 6, 1954 issue of *The Billboard*. I received more than a dozen phone calls the day it appeared. (*BILLBOARD MAGAZINE*)

I included this picture because of what it meant to me at the time. As a 25-year-old who had just returned from Korea, playing with Leo Peeper's band in Des Moines, Iowa, getting a picture with Dagmar was maybe the highlight of the tour! (JACK MELICK)

JIMMY PALMER ORCHESTRA

APRIL 1955

Sat. 9........Peoria, Illinois.....Bay Barn Rt. #4................9-1

Sun. 10........Spring Valley,Ill....Les-Buz Br...................9-1

Mon. 11 ______________________________

Tues.12........Decatur, Ill.........Elks Club......................9-1

Wed. 13........St. Cloud, Wisc......Hollywood Resort Br............9-1

Thurs14........Mt. Horeb, Wisc......Club 18........................9-1

Fri. 15........Monmouth, Ill........Fire Dept......................9-1

Sat. 16........Omaha, Nebraska......Peony Park.....................9-1

Sun. 17........Hatfield, Minn.......Hollyhock Br...................9-1

Mon. 18........Avoca, Iowa..........Avoca Br.......................9-1

Tues.19........Hartley, Iowa........Neehel's Danceland.............9-1

Wed. 20........Silver Lake, Minn....Pla-Mor Br.....................9-1

Thur.21........Spillville, Iowa.....Inwood Br......................9-1

Fri. 22........Davenport, Iowa......Coliseum Br....................9-1

Sat. 23........Ft.Leavenworth, Kans.Officers Open Mess.............9-1

Sun. 24........Norfolk, Neb.........Kings Br.......................9-1

Mon. 25........Salina, Kansas.......Moose Lodge....................9-1

Tues.26........Norton, Kansas.......Silvaire Br....................9-1

Wed. 27 ______________________________

Thur.28........Great Bend,Kansas....Theatre & Am.Legion Bldg. 8 p.m. Theatre 9:30-12:30

Fri. 29........Wichita, Kansas......Trig Br........................9-1

Sat. 30........Wichita, Kansas......Trig Br........................9-1

MAY 1955

Sun. 1........Wichita, Kansas......Trig Br........................9-1

Mon. 2 ______________________________

Tues. 3 ______________________________

Wed. 4 ______________________________

Thurs.5........Yuma, Arizona........ ______________

Fri. 6........Phoenix, Arizona..... ______________

Sat. 7........San Diego, Cal.......Trianon Br.....................9-1

Sun. 8........March AFB,Riverside,Cal....Officers Club...........8-12

Mon. 9 ______________________________

Tues.10Thru22..Hollywood, Cal.......Palladium Br. ______________

Sun. 8........March AFB,Riverside,Cal....Officers Club...

Mon. 9

Tues.10Thru22..Hollywood, Cal.......Palladium Br.

Jimmy Palmer's schedule for April and May of 1955. What caught my eye was the date at the bottom of the schedule! (JACK MELICK)

An impromptu softball game in May 1955 with the Mills Brothers while traveling with Jimmy Palmer's band in Springfield, Illinois... the kind of simple pleasure that has made life extraordinary. (ALL PHOTOS JACK MELICK)

Herb Mills and I wait our turn at bat.

I don't remember why Harry Mills and I seem to be fascinated with these drinks! But we're with Ken, the bartender at the hotel, so.....

Don Mills strolls into third.

Herb Mills chugs home (left), and yeah, my baseball career never amounted to much.

Members of Jimmy's band with Harry Mills; (left to right) Clarence Stuchel, Danny D'Andrea, and Hank Mitchell.

Many decades later, Don Mills and I reconnected at a BBAA convention. He remembered the softball game!

The Jimmy Palmer Orchestra appeared at the Hollywood Palladium in May, 1955. Jimmy Palmer is standing just right of center. You'll find me at the piano far left. (HOLLYWOOD PALLADIUM)

My first commercial big band date with MCA in Boston. I put together a pretty good band of musicians out of Boston for the Statler Hotel, December 1956. (BOSTON PARK PLAZA/ STATLER HOTEL)

After Boston, to the Shamrock Hotel in Houston, 1957. (SHAMROCK HILTON HOTEL)

My name in lights... for the first time, 1957. (JACK MELICK)

OA6 25

O REA476 PD=RENO NEV 11 437PMP=

JACK MELICK=

SKY ROOM MAPES HOTEL RENO NEV=

CONGRATULATIONS HAVE A WONDERFUL ENGAGEMENT BEST WISHES
TO CHARLES AND PEACH FOR A VERY SUCCESSFUL SEASON=

EDDIE FITZPATRICK=..

This congratulatory telegram from Eddie Fitzpatrick, after I took over for him as the house band at the Mapes Hotel, meant so much to me. (JACK MELICK)

The Mapes Hotel in Reno was home for the Jack Melick Orchestra from 1959-1960. The hotel was taken down in 2000. Here's just a small sample of the many stars that graced the stage at the Sky Room. (ALL IMAGES MAPES HOTEL)

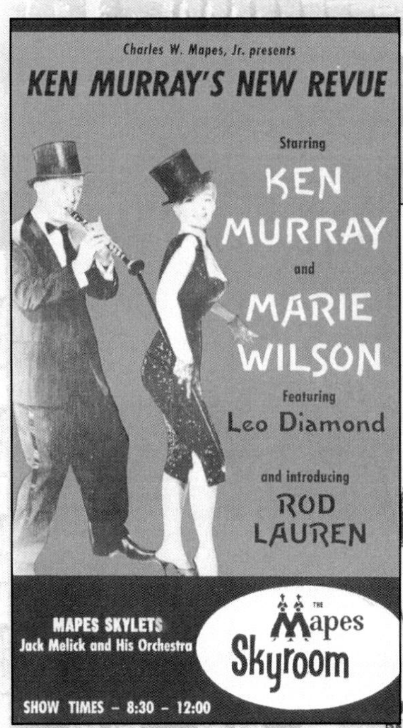

Notice the house band is billed in each ad.

The Far East was always a favorite place to perform, and I returned whenever I could. From 1965-1968, I made the Far East part of my yearly itinerary. I was a regular at the Tachikawa Air Base O-Club (left) and Club Alba in Manila (below).
(JACK MELICK)

Freddy Martin and me at BBAA in the mid-80's. We played at the Ambassador Hotel at the same time. He was the house band in the Cocoanut Grove ballroom, and I was downstairs in the Casino Room. Freddy was the first "big name" to help me out in California. (JACK MELICK)

Orrin Tucker and me at BBAA in the mid-80's. I learned how to be a dance band leader from this man. Orrin lived to be 100 and only recently passed away in 2011. (JACK MELICK)

And then there were two... we didn't know it would be true at the BBAA in the mid-80's, but here in the mid-2010's, Ray Anthony and I may be the last two big band leaders. (JACK MELICK)

Three generations of John T's. Left to right, John T. Melick, III, John T. Melick IV, and John T. Melick, Jr. in 2001. (JACK MELICK)

Found: 50 Years Later

In 1959 and 1960, I was the leader of the house band at the Mapes Hotel in Reno, Nevada. The show room was called the Sky Room. It was an elegant job and we were playing for stars like Milton Berle, Betty Grable, Mickey Rooney, Myron Cohen, and Sammy Davis, Jr. When the big acts came to town, their names were in great big letters in the newspaper ads, of course. Somewhere in the ad, in small type, you would read, "Jack Melick and His Orchestra." So, when the people came into the Sky Room, I just thought I'd let the people know whose band it was!

So I had a tailor in town make a banner that proclaimed "Jack Melick and His Orchestra." There would be no mistaking whose band it was!

It came back beautifully; made of silk, it was black and gold with gold fringe around it. It was very elegant. "Jack Melick" and "Orchestra" were in large cursive letters surrounding "and his" in the middle. I was proud to hang in up on the wall behind the bandstand. It looked great to me. People looking at the band would see that and think, "This must really be a good band. Look at their banner!" My intention was to have it up there the entire 1959-1960 winter season.

Someone else made other plans though, and my display lasted only one night. The second day, we came to work and it wasn't there. I looked all over the stage area, the dressing areas around the stage, and found nothing. I called the cleaning crew. They knew nothing. I talked to the manager, Mr. Mapes. I talked to everybody, and it was just gone. Nobody had any idea where it was. We even ran ads in the paper about it. They ran in both the newspapers for a couple of weeks at least. Nobody ever turned up with that banner.

I mean, nobody in the world needed that banner but me! We continued to ask about it, but it never turned up. Over time, it just faded from our minds and we forgot about it. 1960 and 1961 came and went. I went back on the road, then back to Japan several times, and life continued.

Years go by… well lots of them in fact; about 49 of them to 2008. I got an email that read, "Did you have an orchestra? We have discovered a banner with your name on it. We looked you up on Google and saw your name and email address." It had been so long—almost 50 years—that I had to think about it for a minute! I called them up immediately and said, "Yes I did. That banner belonged to our band and it's been gone for many years."

It seems that her brother had it. He had died recently on Okinawa, of all places. She asked if I had ever been there. Of course, I had played there a couple of times, but never had the banner with me.

She said, "Well, I found it in my brother's belongings. When his stuff arrived home, there was this banner in a box."

I told her I didn't know why he would have it, because he never got it from me. But I'm sure it's mine. She described it, and said her brother was in the Air Force. She asked when it disappeared. I told her that it was at the end of 1959. She said he was stationed at Stead Air Force Base at that time. (Stead Air Force Base is 10 miles north of Reno.)

Somehow, the banner "arrived at the base." She didn't know how. Obviously (or at least it seems obvious to me), some of the troopers from Stead came down to town, drinking in Reno and having fun, maybe went to a show in the Sky Room, saw the banner, had a couple more drinks and said, "Let's go take that banner!"

My guess is that he and his buddies took it as a souvenir. All the years went by. Of course, he couldn't do anything with the banner except hide it. She said he was stationed in Okinawa a couple of times, and apparently, he kept the banner wherever he went. Then he settled in Okinawa.

When he died, everything was shipped back to his family in California. Fifty years later, my banner is unpacked and sees the light of day!

I asked, "Can you send it? Can you ship it to me?" I didn't know if she was going to ask for something. I gave her my address. She just said, "Oh yes. We'll mail it to you."

And so they did. It came wrapped up very nicely. It's raggedy around the edges. It looked like it had been used. I don't know how or why, but it came. And I didn't know if I should send some money or anything, so I sent her a couple of CD's we had done as thanks. I never heard from her again.

So nearly 50 years later, we get out the old banner from time to time and hang it proudly, especially if we're playing a highly social event or big important event. Now I know... this is a really good banner!

And the Beat Still Goes On

At 80-something, I still get to lead the band! (JACK MELICK)

The Jack Melick Orchestra, 2014; Marshall Head, Jeff Richey, Scott Covey, Wesley Smith, Alex Camp, Mark Roberts, Larry Spence, Kelley Fletcher, Scott Marsrow, and Marty Kobuck. Marshall and Wesley have been with me for 50 years. (JACK MELICK)

6
The Next Liberace

MCA Signs the Kid From Jersey

Bob Willding's pitch was that they wanted to make me the next famous band leader. He said, "We think that you could be another Liberace or Carmen Cavallaro." Cavallaro was another famous piano-playing band leader at the time. I'm not sure I swallowed the whole pitch, but MCA was THE agency at the time. It was a great break and perfect timing, so I signed with Music Corporation of America (MCA), and Bob was my agent there.

MCA was the only agent I had ever had. Once I came to Dallas for good, I began to represent myself. I'll write more about that later, but through the late 50's and early 60's, MCA got me a lot of good consistent work as the leader of the band, including a great job as a headliner in Reno.

A Prior Engagement

While I waited for MCA to find me work as a leader, I got an interesting call. An MCA agent told me that Bette Davis was going to be calling me. She wanted a pianist to come play a party for her. They gave her my number.

Sure enough, the next day, the phone rang and it was Bette Davis. Her husband Gary Merrill was having a birthday party. They were having a dinner party at their home for 10 or 12 of his friends. She asked me to play at the party, and of course, I accepted.

She said, "Well, there's one thing I want you to do, and maybe you won't want to do it. I want you to come dressed as a nun."

"Well, Miss Davis," I answered, "I don't happen to have a nun's outfit in my closet."

She said, "I'll call Hollywood Costume, and they'll get out all the stuff that makes up a nun's habit."

Merrill's nickname was "Monk," and she thought it would be funny if, after all his guests were there enjoying cocktails, the doorbell would ring. Merrill would answer the door to a man dressed as a nun who walks in and sits down at the piano to play "Happy Birthday."

She said she'd pay me $100 for that and then to continue to play while they were having dinner. Well, it was 1957, so $100 was good money for someone not real famous playing music for someone who was! So I said okay.

I went and got the stuff, brought it home and put it all on. I looked at myself and thought, oh, my god. Then I thought it would be kind of funny for a 6'-4" man to sit down at the piano and play "Happy Birthday" while dressed as a nun.

So the arrangement was that I would arrive early with the outfit in my suitcase, and she would arrange a room for me to change. I arrived at her house, she took me to one of the bedrooms and said, "Stay back here and get dressed. The guests are going to be here soon, and my husband's not home yet. I'll come back and get you."

So I got dressed in Bette Davis's bedroom in a nun's outfit. And it must have been an hour or more until everyone had arrived. She came back and got me, and led me through the kitchen and out the back. I walked around her house in this nun's outfit and knocked on the front door.

I heard her shout, "I'm in the kitchen, Gary. Can you

get it for me?"

So, he came to the door and there I was. And I said, "Can I come in, Monk?"

He answered, "Well, yes." He was a little more than startled!

I walked directly over to the piano and sat down. I gave a quick glance to the guests at the table, and counted, "a one, two, three, four!" and we all went into "Happy Birthday." There I was... playing "Happy Birthday" at the piano in a nun's outfit. I don't have a picture of it. I wish I did, but at least I still have the order form from Hollywood Costume.

After an hour or so, I was getting a little warm. So, Bette came over and she said, "You can go back and change into your regular clothes now. I know you must be getting hot in that outfit."

She was very nice. So I went back, changed clothes, and came back and played again until the dinner party was over. They seemed to enjoy the music I was playing—the popular music of the day, just softly in the background, which I could do. But in a nun's outift... now, that was different!

The Game of Darts

There's an old story that booking offices get out a map of the United States and throw darts at it to determine where you're going to end up. Well, the first dart hit Boston, Massachusetts. I had not put a band together since my military days, and they came up with a three-month engagement for a big band starting in the first week of December through the first of March; wintertime in Boston.

Problem was that I was living in Hollywood. So, I'm

in southern California and I have to get a band of 11 people together who will go to Boston in the wintertime, over the holidays no less, with a leader they don't even know.

Right, no problem!

Well, it meant that I was going to get guys who couldn't really play. I ended up with a bunch of misfits. No one was very good. We opened on December 3, 1956 at the Statler Hotel. I remember that day because it was the day of the Boston College – Holy Cross football game. There was a big traffic jam in downtown Boston.

Well, of course, we weren't very good. But after the first one-month engagement, my contract was renewed. They renewed it every month, in fact, even though I was having problems, because I became good friends with the manager. He understood I was having trouble getting good musicians. I had to let half the ones go that I had brought to Boston, so there were only 5 of the original group left.

I also had to fire the singer that had been supplied to me in New York by MCA. She was a terrific singer, but the old Boston money that frequented the Statler at that time did not like her. She wore a lot of petticoats and when she sat on a stool she showed a lot of leg.

This didn't go over too well with the Beacon Hill crowd. I ended up with a girl from Boston who wore long dresses instead of petticoats! They never saw her legs, but could she sing!

We actually finished up with an excellent band because the guys were all from Boston. They had gone to the Berklee School of Music and the New England Conservatory of Music. They were terrific musicians, and were glad to get a six-nights-a-week job. I actually ended up with a great band.

Then the booking office got out the darts again, and the next one hit Houston, Texas. "Jack, you are going to Houston to play at the Shamrock Hotel." Well, of course I had a new problem—the guys I hired in Boston wouldn't go all the way to Texas!

After three months of hard work bringing along one set of guys, I had to start all over again. I went to a union hiring hall in New York City. It was Union local 802. I walked up on stage and announced, "I need a third alto saxophone player and a first trumpet player willing to go to Houston." It was another three-month job, but many guys volunteered to go because they weren't working. I auditioned guys and went down to Houston all set with a pretty good band—or at least that's what I thought!

When I got to Houston there was a message for me that the first trumpet player I had hired in New York had changed his mind about coming to Houston. It was the day before we opened and we were having a rehearsal the next morning with the DeCastro Sisters. So I called around Houston. The substitute turned out to be E. C. Holland, the best lead trumpet player in Houston.

Our lead alto sax, Ray Repkay, was also from New York, and he got on the phone and called the missing trumpet player. He told him, "You gotta come down here. Jack's in a real hole down here. You can't just quit with one day's notice." I guess he really gave him the dickens over the phone. So he talked the guy into coming down. A few days later he showed up in Houston after all.

But what a nice four days it was listening to E. C.

Holland play every night!

Shep Fields led the band that was there before us. Fields was a very well known band leader from the big band era, and I had known about him since I was a kid and always wanted to hear him play. So I went to his last night with the Houston MCA agent. After his show, he sat down with us.

I told him how happy I was to meet him and then began to describe the escapade I had with my trumpet player. He looked at me and said, "Don't tell me about it. You wanted to be a band leader didn't you? I've had these troubles for 50 years. This is what happens." Of course he was absolutely right. It was an early reminder for me about being a band leader!

The next dart hit Phoenix, Arizona. So it went from L.A. to Boston to Houston to Phoenix. Let's see if we can get these a little farther apart! I'm making my way back around to the west coast.

I get booked in Phoenix at a place called the Flame Restaurant. This was not a big band job, but the Flame Restaurant was an interesting place. Phoenix was not a big metropolis like it is now, so we started at 6:00 PM to catch the work crowd. They had a bar there with a jungle background. They even had a monkey.

It was actually pretty jumpin' from 6 to 10 when we played there. I went back to the Flame Restaurant on three different occasions.

Between the engagements in Boston, Houston and Phoenix, I played at the Ambassador Hotel in Los Angeles from time to time. The big room was called the Cocoanut Grove where Freddy Martin's band played. I played downstairs in the Casino Room. My trio consisted of my old drummer David Alpert and a bass player named Jack Kennedy. It was a Hollywood hangout so a lot of movie stars would show up to hear us play.

I remember Jack Lemmon walking up and standing beside the piano while I played. He was a pianist himself—played jazz—so I asked, "Do you want to sit in?"

He said, "No, no, just listening to you." He came in several times.

I also saw Jerry Lewis and even more stars. They would come in and hang out and have drinks.

My Name in Lights

The Casino Room was an important place in developing my name. It was also the first time I saw my name up in lights. Guy Lombardo came to play at the Cocoanut Grove, so on the front of the Ambassador Hotel was his name, "Guy Lombardo and His Orchestra." But down below Lombardo's name was mine, "Casino Dancing Jack Melick Trio" in lights. It was all show biz and egotism, but obviously a huge moment in my career.

Would You Like to Go to Reno?

By the end of 1957, MCA was doing a great job putting me to work in some really nice engagements. I joke about the "dart board," but going to places like Boston, Houston, Phoenix and back to L.A. was really establishing me as a top working band leader and performer. Sometimes it was with a big band, and other times it might be with a trio or even solo on the piano. Then, early in 1958, they got me a foothold in one of the most important live music markets in the western part of the United States at that time.

Those were the days when there was still live music in all of the casinos. It was wonderful. Live music everywhere. And the casinos were mainly in two towns—Las Vegas and Reno, Nevada.

One of the top spots was the Mapes Hotel and Casino in Reno. MCA said they had a job for me there with a trio in the Mapes Casino Lounge. They needed an instrumental group that would play early in the afternoon for the people getting off from work. It was all quiet, happy, and familiar cocktail music.

So, I went to Reno with a trio for another three months—piano, bass, and drums. We played from 4:00 in the afternoon until 10:00. Around 8:00, we would begin to alternate with another group that would continue on until midnight. Then at 10:00, as we were knocking off, they would alternate with another group that would go from 10:00 until 2:00 or 4:00 in the morning. So, the Casino Lounge had live music from 4:00 P.M. until 4:00 A.M. every day.

We'd play whatever we wanted, and of course, we took requests. It was a cocktail lounge, so people would write down their requests on a cocktail napkin and send them on up! Of course, I preferred if they wrote the tune on a $20 bill and sent it up instead, but either way, we played what the people wanted us to play.

After doing that for three months, I went back home to L.A. But it wouldn't be my last visit to Reno. In fact, that little job would soon turn into something much, much bigger!

But for now, this was the life I lived as a traveling

musician. I often found myself back at the Ambassador Hotel in L.A. at the Casino Room. There were dates in Albuquerque and back in Hollywood at Jerry Lewis's restaurant. All of it was a great experience. I took every job, and I wanted to do everything. It added up to being able to make a living in a time when the music business wasn't good to everybody, but I could do whatever needed to be done.

Well, after that first trip back to L.A., I got a call from MCA to head right back to the Mapes Hotel in Reno. It seems that Charles Mapes himself has requested that I come back and play the early shift again in the Casino Lounge.

The Sky Room

Now in these days, most of the top hotels had a main ballroom or show room where they would book big-name entertainment. Each ballroom had a "house band," led by the band leader as the headliner. Then they would have one or more lounges where smaller groups like trios or individual performers would play in a more casual atmosphere.

The headliners at the more prestigious hotels became pretty famous themselves. The Ambassador Hotel in Los Angeles was a good example. The headliner at the Ambassador's Cocoanut Grove ballroom was Freddy Martin. He and his band would have their own performances, but would also back up famous singers or comedians in their performances.

Naturally, the Cocoanut Grove in the heart of L.A. would have the best entertainment available. Then down in the lounge, called the Casino Room, they would have an excellent group like the Jack Melick Trio keeping the lounge goers entertained for late-night cocktails or before big performances in the Cocoanut Grove. In fact, some of my best times were those engagements in the Casino Room when Freddy Martin and Hollywood celebrities would come in and watch us play.

The ballroom at the Mapes Hotel in Reno was on the top floor and it was called the Sky Room. By the summer of 1959, I had now played several engagements in the Casino Lounge downstairs.

Mr. Mapes was going to close the Sky Room during the summer of 1959. Then he was going to re-open it in the fall and stay open indefinitely with the Winter Olympics of 1960 coming to Squaw Valley in February just outside of Reno. And anticipating the big audiences, he was going to have big acts coming in.

The headliner in the Sky Room, since about 1949 or so, was a San Francisco band leader named Eddie Fitzpatrick. Eddie had a full-time band, and when Mr. Mapes decided to close for the summer, he couldn't afford to take the summer off. Eddie found a year-round, full-time job across the street in Reno at the Riverside Hotel. Eddie and his guys became the permanent band there. Bill Clifford, leader of their current band was retiring to Phoenix.

So, as the time to re-open the Sky Room neared, Charles Mapes needed a band. Mr. Mapes turned to MCA. Bobby Burns, who formerly was the manager for Tommy Dorsey and other name bands, was still an agent at MCA. He was older now, of course, but he was still handling performers for Mr. Mapes, including me.

He told Mr. Mapes that I had the experience in places

like Boston and Houston, and had always wanted to lead my own big band. Mr. Mapes knew me very well from the Casino Lounge, and had personally requested I come back there.

Still, Mr. Mapes hesitated and then called Eddie Fitzpatrick, his former band leader.

Eddie told him, "Jack would be perfect for you." So the old band leader recommended me as well as my agent, Bobby Burns. That was good enough for him, so Mr. Mapes called me and we made a deal. The Jack Melick Orchestra, at least in name at this point, was officially born!

This time I got really good guys. I put my band together entirely out of L.A. I was much more experienced and knew whom to call this time around. I played in the Sky Room all through the Olympics, through the following summer, and into the next year. The Jack Melick Orchestra was now the house band in the Sky Room at the Mapes Hotel in Reno, Nevada!

Advertisements for the hotel would include "Jack Melick and His Orchestra" along with famous names such as Milton Berle, Myron Cohen, Sammy Davis Jr., Betty Grable, Mickey Rooney, and a host of others that would appear during that wonderful year. This was a major turning point in my career. I established a reputation within the entertainment business because I played with these famous people (even though you usually had to search the ads for my name).

Being the House Band

Being a house band involved a lot of routine. Like other show rooms, the Sky Room had a chorus line. Chorus lines need music. There were eight chorus girls and two chorus guys. It was a pretty big troupe. They were called the Mapettes or something like that.

Then, every show would have two acts; the opening act and the star. At least one of them was always musical. Many nights, both of them were music acts. So the band was a necessity. Besides, the Reno musicians union also had rules that these large hotels had to have at least ten musicians working at all times in the showrooms.

The non-musical acts like the comedians still had musical needs too. The comedians all wanted on and off music. I'd say, "Ladies and gentlemen, Shecky Greene!" And the band played him on. Just like *The Tonight Show*!

Other comics like Milton Berle also used music throughout their routines. Music was part of their act. Whenever Milton called for a "clyde," I played one, and he'd start to sing, "There's just one place for me... Near You..." That was his theme song. The "clyde" was an arpeggio, and the name given to me by Uncle Miltie was "Mr. Greenbaum." I have no idea why.

The rest of the time, we were just sitting there and laughing. And if it wasn't funny, we didn't laugh.

A Rising "Star"

For most of my career to this point, I had been an itinerant musician. This was a long-time gig of more than a year. Still, I never knew—I was still on the journey. So I had no idea where I really wanted to end up or how it was going to end up.

I wouldn't have made any permanent arrangements in Reno anyway because I didn't get the feeling that this is the place I wanted to settle in. In those days, we found a nice apartment where they'd take 30 days notice. We didn't sign a lease for a year, or pay first and last month's rent. We just stayed in there until the job was over. That's what we did. I had a nice apartment there and just stayed in that for the whole time. And at that time, I knew that my wife and new baby might be with me for some of the time, so I got a nicer apartment. I was playing at the Sky Room when my son, John T. Melick III, was born.

But this was my first close, personal contact with the people that I had heard of and admired or idolized all my life. And they accepted me as one of them.

The Mapes Hotel coffee shop had a Chinese menu that went on about midnight. And many a night I would be sitting down there with George Gobel, Milton Berle, Vic Damone, or another of these famous people. There we'd be just sitting around having Chinese food and talking. When I was sitting with a star like Milton Berle, other comedians that were working in town or at Lake Tahoe, would come in and join us. These comic greats were all sitting around telling stories. And I'm sitting there laughing all night. They were telling me all their stories, and it was some really great times. I was a great audience!

So anyway, the good times must sometime end. Well, not for good, but at least in Reno.

Ken Murray

In the fall of 1959, the Jack Melick Orchestra opened

for the first time in the Sky Room with Ken Murray and his "All New Blackouts." Murray had been famous for a long time on radio and TV with a show called *The Ken Murray Blackouts*. He was a well-known comedian and you never saw him without his cigar.

"Blackout" meant literally that—when you had a funny moment in a skit, maybe somebody's pants dropped, the band hit a big chord and all the lights went out... you know, a blackout! So Ken Murray's variety show was composed of a lot of skits, and he had a large-bosomed woman on the show. Marie Wilson was of minimal talent, but that wasn't why she was there anyway. She was the classic "dumb blond" with large boobs, and that's what Ken liked.

He paid me one of the highest compliments. "The thing I like about this band is that you are very alert, and that's important in the entertainment business." I always remembered that. He meant my band was always ready to play or improvise or react to the act on stage.

I mentioned his cigars. Every once in a while, he would see me in the hall, lay twenty bucks down and say, "Go buy your daughter a cigar." I picked that up over the years. When I would get tips from the audience, I would give the guys five or 10 bucks and say, "Buy your daughter a cigar!"

Jan Murray

The very next show was with another comedian named Murray; Jan Murray (no relation to Ken). He was a great guy, and I had a wonderful experience doing his show, but what I will remember most is that he stole our singer!

He was starting a new television game show called Treasure Hunt and he needed an assistant—just think of Vanna White on today's *Wheel-of-Fortune*. He made our singer Marian Stafford his first "Pirate Girl."

Lili St. Cyr

Another interesting act we played for was Lili St. Cyr. She was the foremost burlesque act of the time. She had gone beyond the funky old burlesque theaters onto the mainstream stage. This was not a strip joint!

Normally, the band would be at the back of the stage. That's where we played when we accompanied a comedy act, singers, or dancers. When she was there, though, they moved the whole band over to one of the wings and put a curtain across so the band couldn't see her act.

First of all, she didn't want people behind her watching her do this act taking a bath in big cocktail glass. But most of all, she had this secret. She wore flesh-colored clothing. From the audience, it looked like she was nude, but the band would know that she was all covered up.

But in order to play the tunes she wanted, I had to watch her. So I had to peep through the curtains to know when she went to another part of her routine as her music needed to change. I'd fade the band out and bring them in on the next tune. We'd play beautiful, romantic, sexy tunes like "The Barefoot Contessa," "Fascination," and "The Lamp is Low."

After her bathing routine, which was the final act, she'd run off the opposite wing soaking wet. The PR guy from the hotel, Harry Spencer, had to be back there in the wings with a great big towel. When she got into the wings, he wrapped her up in the towel and escorted her back to her room. We always told Harry that his main job at the Mapes Hotel was to wrap Lili St. Cyr in a towel and take her back to her room!

Mickey Rooney

Mickey Rooney had an act with Joey Foreman and it was one of the funniest acts I had ever seen. We just screamed with laughter every night, even though we saw the same act twice a night for two weeks! Mickey would also play the drums in his act. He was a pretty good drummer.

When he was playing in the Sky Room, the Winter Olympics had started. I drove Mickey and his wife to Squaw Valley for the games during the daytime. Of course, the performances were at night. He had an infant at the time who's now in his mid-50s. I often wonder where he is or what he's doing. Anyway, Mickey was a real nice man, and I had a good time with him.

Myron Cohen

Myron Cohen was a very well known comedian. He had been on *The Ed Sullivan Show* numerous times and told wonderful stories. Myron used my band only for coming on and going off stage. So during the middle of the show of course, we were just sitting there, laughing up a storm.

However, every once and a while, right in the middle

of his act, he would turn around and say, "Jack, I need more saxes and violins!" And of course, we had not played a note for half an hour! We were all just sitting there with our legs crossed and laughing. It was a great time.

We became very close, and my son, John Melick III, was born at the time he was there. He was born back home in Los Angeles, and my wife at the time brought the baby up to Reno.

I have a nice picture of Myron Cohen holding the baby while they were here. We had a softball game where my band played the band from the Riverside Hotel. Cohen came out. He was our coach while he was carrying my son around. That was a great day! That baby has become a director in the film industry.

Billy Eckstine and Don Rickles

Billy Eckstine was a famous jazz singer. He formed his own big band and it was a jumping-off point for greats like Dizzy Gillespie, Miles Davis, Charlie Parker, and Sarah Vaughan. He sang so well that he broke up his band and became a solo performer, a very good one with lots of big selling records.

When he did his act in the Sky Room, he told me, "Your band plays really well in tune. It's really nice to work with you." To the non-musical ear, that may not sound like much, but that was a huge compliment. Believe it or not, some bands—especially the horns—are not accurately playing in tune. And sometimes they don't even know it! Eckstine played terrific trombone and trumpet before he started singing exclusively, so he knew if the guys were playing in tune. So it was a compliment to be told the band is really playing in tune.

At the time of his visit, Don Rickles and Sarah Vaughan were across the street at The Riverside. I went over there one night and was sitting in the bar. There was Sarah Vaughan sitting there. I introduced myself, and sat down with her. I told her she was an idol of mine when I was in high school. She didn't look much different this time than she did that time I saw her at Birdland in New York as a teenager.

I was talking to her when Don Rickles came out and sat down with us, too. We all know his trademark act insulting people, so after we talked for a little while, he said, "Jack, this is not Las Vegas, you know, where there are hotels up and down the Strip, and there are lots of famous people for me to feed off of and insult in my act. Could you get Billy Eckstine to come over and catch my show?"

We laughed, but I was extremely flattered at this, you know. Here was this big-time comedian asking me if I could make an arrangement for him. This was still my first big-time engagement, and these stars were all treating me very nicely. So I said, "yeah... I bet I can!"

I talked to Billy the next day about it. I told him that Don Rickles and Sarah Vaughan would like him to come over and see the show. He answered, "Okay, let's go."

After his show the next night, we went across the street and caught the late show at the Riverside. Rickles saw Billy Eckstine in the audience. The first time he saw him, he said, "Well, Billy Eckstine is here. I remember when you were a High Yellow from east Texas," or something like that.

That was the opening line. It went down hill from there! And Billy loved it. The celebrities loved to get insulted by Rickles. (He never insulted me of course. I wasn't famous enough, even though I did deliver Billy Eckstine.) That was a fun experience.

Milton Berle

One of the best stars I ever worked with was Milton Berle. He was five years old when he started in his parents' Vaudeville act and I was helping him break in a new act celebrating his 50th anniversary in show business. He was breaking it in in Reno, and he was going to go to New Orleans with it after he finished with us.

I played the piano for his act and helped him with the cues for the band members. And he took a big liking to me. For some reason he started calling me Mr. Greenbaum. As I wrote earlier, he also had a word for the musical term "arpeggio." An arpeggio is just a series of notes played one at a time. He called it a "clyde." I have no idea where these came from, and I never asked him either!

So in the middle of the show he would say to me, "Mr. Greenbaum, give me a clyde!" He would do this three or four times during a show, and I would play an arpeggio because I knew what the next song was going to be. It was all charted out. I worked very closely with him and he paid me a hundred extra because I would meet with him on my own time to work this stuff out.

After Reno, he left for New Orleans with his fine-tuned 50th anniversary act. Three or four days after he was gone, my phone rings at 4:00am. It's Milton. He said, "Jack—" He didn't call me Mr. Greenbaum this time, so I knew something was up.

"Jack, this is Milton. I need a drummer, and I want Russ."

Russ Patrick was my drummer. He was a very good drummer, especially backing shows.

"Russ played a great show," Milton said. "I can't get a drummer like that down here that can play a great show like that. I want Russ. Can I have him?"

He didn't say "please," but I answered, "Well, I can't stop you from hiring him, but what are you going to pay?"

"$350 a week plus transportation and expenses," Milton said. "Russ is so precise. When I turn around and my pants fall down, he hits a rimshot just when my pants hit the floor! He can do old-fashioned schtick, or burlesque, or show business stuff. He's a very fine show drummer and I want to hire him."

So I called Russ in the morning, and told him what Milton had told me. I told Russ I certainly wouldn't stop him, and that I couldn't pay that kind of salary. I don't remember what I was paying, but it certainly wasn't at the Milton Berle level.

Russ was a local Reno guy, and this was 1960. Needless to say, Russ joined Milton Berle in New Orleans and stayed with him for quite awhile I think. I eventually lost track of Russ Patrick.

Well, I remember that I had done the same thing way back when. This time I had to experience it from the band leader's side. That day I started calling around and found a local musician, Roger Ward, who was a well-known show drummer. He was available, came on board, and played the rest of our stay there. He did a great job.

Sammy Davis, Jr.

I also had a couple of difficult experiences in Reno. Thee two I remember were with Sammy Davis Jr. and Betty Grable.

Sammy was a great talent, of course, and his uncle, Will Mastin, would always sit out in the audience. He started out with his father and uncle in the Will Mastin Trio. Sammy broke out on his own and became a big star, of course. One night, early in his two-week engagement in the Sky Room, Sammy came out and sang only four tunes. After he sang "That Old Black Magic," he walked off the stage. I didn't know why, but I led the applause figuring he'd come back out to do another three or four songs. He never came back out.

Well, I was still pretty young and wasn't thinking. I said to the audience, "Well, it seems the star has decided not to sing for us any more tonight. So we'll start with some dance music." And we invited everyone to dance. People came up and danced, but it was a short show that evening.

Later, I was sitting out in the lobby having a beer, and our PR guy comes over. His name was Ty Tyson and he told me, "Sammy wants to see you in his dressing room."

I had a hunch what it was about of course, so before I went down, I went to see Mr. Mapes who was also in the bar area. I told him that Sammy had only done four songs and that I made a sarcastic remark to the audience about it.

"His uncle was in the audience and had obviously told him about it. He wants to see me in his dressing room. What should I do about it?"

Mr. Mapes said, "Well, you'd better go, but he has nothing to do with you. He works directly for me. So if he wants to complain, he'll have to complain to me about it. He can't do anything like fire you. So don't worry about that. You're my band leader, and I'm not going to fire you.

"But you were in the wrong, and you had better go back there and talk to him about it." So I did, knowing that Sammy couldn't get me fired. But of course, he was right about our dispute. He was really mad.

"It's not your place to criticize me over the microphone, or be sarcastic about me," he said. "You are the band leader here. You're not my boss. You didn't sign any contracts with me. You just play the music. You were out of line."

We talked for a long time. He was angry, and I just agreed with everything he said. And then we didn't talk for the rest of the two weeks he was there.

What I didn't know was that Sammy had a clause in his contract that there would be no serving while he was on stage. Evidently, a waiter showed up at a ringside table and Sammy heard him taking orders and delivering drinks. He got mad and walked off the stage.

It was between him and Mr. Mapes. I was not involved until I got myself involved. Sammy had that reputation of being a prima donna, but a contract was a contract. In fact, many of the entertainers had clauses like that. It was completely logical. Everything had to be just right. I took full responsibility and learned a hard lesson.

Betty Grable

When Betty Grable came to Reno, she had closed the night before in Las Vegas. She caught an early plane because she had to open the next night at the Sky Room. Mr. Mapes and Ty Tyson met her at the Reno airport, and before they could even say, "Welcome to Reno," she said, "Why didn't anybody tell me it was so goddamn cold up here?"

So she was already in a bad mood—not enough sleep and too much cold.

Rehearsals were at 10:00 and 2:00 for an opening that night. We're playing a piece of special material that I think was based on her failed relationship with Harry James. The name of it was "I'd Rather Bet on a Horse Than a Man," or something like that. Anyway, I'm conducting it and playing the piano part when she suddenly stops in the middle of the tune.

She turned on me and said, "Jack, are you going to conduct or play the piano?"

"Well, I usually do both. I conduct from the piano," I said. I had been there more than a year doing that.

"I don't want you do to both," she said. "Either conduct the show or play the piano, not both."

"Well, I'll have to get somebody," I replied.

She said, "Get somebody then." So I called a break in the rehearsal, and went to see Mr. Mapes. It was his decision since I didn't have the money in my contract to hire another musician. I told him she didn't think I could do both, and wanted me to concentrate on one thing. I asked him what he wanted me to do.

He said, "Go find one—pianist or conductor—whichever you think is best, and we'll pay for it. Don't worry about it." So I knew a guy in Reno who was a really good accompanist but not a good band leader. He wasn't a soloist but was an expert at doing shows. He was available, came over at 2:00, and jumped right in at the piano. I conducted. We did the whole two weeks like that.

At the end of the two weeks, Grable gave me some gold cufflinks and a tie clip. A note with the gift said she was sorry we got off to such a bad start. I still have the note and the cufflinks.

This might not seem like a big deal to some, but she was a very famous woman. When I was a teenager she was the queen of the "pin-up girls." Every guy overseas in the army had a picture of her in his locker. I had seen all her movies and then to have her get nasty with me was very upsetting. Even on opening night, I felt terrible and got sick between shows that night.

I ended up calling the Riviera Hotel in Las Vegas where she had just played previously. I wanted to talk to the band leader there. His name was Jack Cathcart. I identified myself to him on the phone and told him my story about Betty Grable—from getting off the plane in a bad mood to being nasty with me because I was, in her eyes, trying to do two jobs.

He said, "Jack, join the club!" Cathcart told me she had given him the same routine—nasty to the band leader and short with the band members. He assured me it wasn't my fault. This made me feel better of course. Anyway, we chalked it up to being an aging, wartime movie star.

7
Life After Reno

On the Road Again

My time in Reno ended when Mr. Mapes decided to close the Sky Room. He thought it was not making enough money. We finished out the year after the Olympics were over and then he shut it down. I joined Milton Berle in New Orleans for two weeks and conducted for him until his regular conductor arrived. Then I went home to Los Angeles.

I started playing dates, with my trio, at familiar places such as the Casino Room in the Ambassador Hotel and Jerry Lewis's new restaurant on Sunset Boulevard. Since MCA was Lewis's agent also, they hired me to play there for three months. Jerry Lewis was a difficult person to work with, and he was nasty to people all over the club. But it was a nice job, a beautiful place, and he actually never treated me badly.

During this time, I also played at a couple of clubs located on California's high desert; the Apple Valley Inn and the Hesperia Inn. I played for Jeri Southern at the Hesperia Inn. She was a marvelous singer and one of my idols in my mid-twenties. Also at the Hesperia Inn, I played for Huntz Hall who had been one of the Dead End Kids; the movie characters that later became known as the Bowery Boys. The group had broken up and Hall was doing his own act. He would tell stories, but he wasn't too funny and was never a huge success in that career.

At the Apple Valley Inn, my band alternated with Billy Regis's band. Billy is the man who recorded the famous trumpet solo on "Cherry Pink and Apple Blossom White" with Perez Prado's band.

"Jack, This is Guy"

I was back in Los Angeles after these shows ended when the phone rang at 4:00 one Saturday morning. I heard a voice say, "Jack, this is Guy." I knew immediately it was Guy Lombardo. I had heard that voice on radio and television so often that I recognized it right then and there. He told me that one of his pianists (he had two pianists) fell on the ice at Lake Tahoe and broke his leg. "We won't have him for several months. I got your name from Freddy Martin. He recommended you. Are you available?"

I said, "Yes, I just finished at Apple Valley and Hesperia."

Guy told me what my pay would be, and it was darn good for 1960! He told me he would have a plane ticket waiting for me at LAX. I would fly to meet the band in Reno. "You can start tonight," he said.

I said, "Mr. Lombardo—" He told me to call him "Guy."

So I said, "Guy, what happens if I don't play well enough for you? You have never heard me play. What would happen if I came to Reno and you found out that I didn't play well enough to make it? Will you pay my way back home if I don't make it?

All he said was, "Do you have a red coat?"

"Yes," I replied.

He said, "You'll make it!"

Guy knew that with Hugo Di Appolito, his other piano player, it didn't really matter how good I could play! Most importantly, I needed to look okay. So, I located my red dinner jacket, "Royal Canadians" crest not included. I didn't have the crest, but I had the red jacket. Off I went to LAX, and to Reno, to meet Guy Lombardo and his Royal Canadians.

Like he said, I played that night and without a rehearsal. We were at Harrah's. The second night at rehearsal, the Lombardo brothers started arguing. There were four of them actually; Liebert, Carmen, Victor, and of course, Guy. They started yelling at each other and calling each other names. I'm sitting there, not at all understanding what is going on. I guess I looked a little worried because the band manager came over and told me they do this all the time. "They're from an old Italian family. They yell and get mad all the time, but they love each other."

I felt much better after that, and it took me only a couple of days to get comfortable playing. I knew just what Guy wanted. I loved the big band dance music when most of my contemporaries were more jazz oriented. Every once in a while, he would look over at me and say, "Yeah... Jack."

Sometimes, when we were on the road, he would call me at 1 or 2 in the morning. He would ask me to go downstairs and have a couple of drinks with him. He wanted to talk about the band business since he knew I wanted to be a band leader. We would drink, and I would get half-loaded! I would go to bed and have to be up early since the bus would leave at 8:00am. I would have to drag myself to the bus, my eyes half open.

Guy, on the other hand, would walk out of the hotel with a big smile, say, "Good morning everybody," and get on the bus shouting, "Let's go!" He looked terrific! I'll never know how he did it!

His brother Liebert played first trumpet. Carmen was playing lead alto. Carmen was really the musician of the family. He wrote famous songs like "Return to Me," "Sweethearts on Parade," and "Boo Hoo," among others, and made a lot of money as a songwriter. He also directed the rehearsals where the big fights among the brothers would start! Victor was the youngest. He was playing the fourth saxophone and didn't join in the shouting.

The second pianist, whom I replaced, was Fred Kreitzer. He was originally from Germany and had emigrated to Canada where he joined Guy Lombardo's band in 1926.

When Hitler came to power a few years later, the band members began calling him "Enemy." When I was traveling with the band—this was 1960—I noticed that some of the old piano parts were labeled "Enemy" in the upper left-hand corner. It was fun to see that the old parts didn't read "piano," or "number 233," or whatever. They read "Enemy" even though the war was long over by this time. But I never got that the others calling him "Enemy" offended Kreitzer. It was just the personality of that war generation.

Several bands tried to imitate Guy Lombardo. Two of them were Jan Garber and Blue Barron, but they were never the same as Lombardo's band. His band was the only one I ever heard that played the melody and people would dance to the melody of the song, rather than the beat. The drummer only tapped a little bit on the side of the drum just to keep everybody together.

Guy Lombardo did not use a string bass. He used a tuba. A string bass and drums are the basic rhythm instruments along with the piano. But the only instrument playing the rhythm in Guy Lombardo's band was the second piano, and that was me, accompanied by the tapping of the drum. The people would fill the dance floor anyway, not listening to the beat.

Lawrence Welk became famous because of his dance beat. You could get on the dance floor and hear that pulse. There was no pulse with Guy Lombardo, but you knew what song it was all the time and you heard a melody. Guy would announce the song. He would turn around and start moving his baton slowly through the air. Yet none of the musicians were looking at him! Carmen would stomp the floor once, and the musicians would count to themselves. They knew what the tempo was supposed to be since they had been with Guy Lombardo for twenty years or longer.

My first night with them was a show, not a dance. Guy raised his baton, I heard a boom, and the band started to play. I quickly caught on, but I asked Hugo later that night how everyone knew when to start, since Guy was not doing anything musically.

"We have all been here so long, we know exactly how fast it is supposed to be and we only need someone to give us the downbeat," Hugo told me. Lombardo's band was the only one I ever played with, or even heard of, that you did not hear a beat. It was just there in the air somewhere!

I didn't watch Guy so much as a leader, but I watched just how the band worked, and how they behaved on the stage. The musicians were all older guys by that time. They owned hardware stores in New York or music stores on Long Island. They were all independently wealthy. For six months of the year, the band would go on the road. For the other six months, they played at the Hotel Roosevelt in New York City.

When I was traveling with them, I talked to them all

and watched. They were very cool. They were not hipsters or jazz monsters. They were guys who knew exactly what they were doing. They knew what the people liked and they knew how to behave on the road.

Guy Lombardo had a rule that the musicians could not drink until the last intermission, which was usually around midnight or 12:30. Then the bar filled up with red coats, and all of the regular customers at the dance were crowded out. All of the guys obeyed his rule and did not drink until then. I guess he figured that a drink at the last intermission was okay, and the guys would not get drunk in 10 minutes.

He was very happy with me and I stayed with him for about 6 months. Before I started working for Guy, MCA had booked me to open at the Chaparral Club in Dallas with my own group. Guy knew I had the contract, but he still wanted me to stay with his band until Fred Kreitzer could return. I told him that I had to go, due to the contract, and he completely understood.

So, I left Guy Lombardo and his Royal Canadians in December 1960 and went to Dallas. He wished me the very best and told me to use his name at any time. I mention him in my publicity, writing that I am "a former member of Guy Lombardo's band."

The Chaparral Club

The Chaparral Club opened in late 1960. Ralph Flanagan and his band came down from New York to play for the grand opening engagement at the club. My band was the second group to play there. We started in late December 1960 and played there three to four months a year.

The Chaparral Club was a private club on the 36th and 37th floors of the Southland Life building in downtown Dallas. It was the first elegant private club to be housed at the top of a Dallas skyscraper.

It was opened primarily as a luncheon club for the officers of Southland Life Insurance Company until it was discovered that people liked to come downtown at night. So, the club began to stay open for dinner and dancing.

There was a spectacular view from the club. The club shared the 37th floor with a very successful restaurant called the "Ports O' Call." Steven Crane, the former husband of Lana Turner, owned the restaurant. Mr. Crane also owned the world famous Luau Restaurant in Hollywood.

Just as Dallas was coming into its own, I met many prominent Dallasites at the club. I got to know R. L. (Bob) Thornton, Jr., John Stemmons, Ben Carpenter of Southland Life, Tom Landry and Tex Schramm. I also came to know Harwood K. Smith, a world-famous architect, Tom Hill of Sun Oil, Cecil Green of Texas Instruments, Dick Blair of Jones-Blair Paints, and many others.

As the years went along, many of them would urge me to settle in Dallas. Established band leaders Joe Reichman and Herman Waldman took me to lunch in downtown Dallas. They welcomed me to Dallas and also urged me to make Dallas my home base.

After a year or so of performing at the Chaparral, I was invited to dinner by some of these prominent Dallasites. They asked if I would stay in Dallas, and they offered to help me in any way they could. Joe Reichman, who played most of the society events in Dallas, was slowing down, and they felt there was a permanent slot opening for me and my band. As we were discussing my musical future in Dallas after dinner, I made the biggest social blunder of my life.

By this time, I had made my first LP record. I just happened to have a pile of those with me, and offered them to my hosts for $5.00 each. They were very gracious and purchased the records. Only later did I think what a foolish mistake it was to sell them. I should have given one to each of my hosts as a souvenir of our wonderful evening!

Well, I played annually at the Chaparral Club for 34 years until it closed in 1994. This was in spite of the fact that I charged for my records at a dinner in my honor.

I Can Travel

By the early 1960's, after my wonderful time in Reno, I was on the road again. I left Guy Lombardo's band, and found myself at the Chaparral Club in Dallas. I had the idea that maybe Dallas would become something of a new home base, replacing Los Angeles, so I rented an apartment there. I would arrange rent for three to four months— however long I would be at the Chaparral Club.

But I never said, "I can't travel." I realized that I had to travel... and own a tux. So I would take the job no matter where it was. And I would bring my musicians with me. Marshall Head, Wesley Smith, and Mark Roberts were on some of those engagements. More than 50 years later, those three are still with me.

So now it was the Chaparral Club on a regular basis in the fall. In the winter and spring, we'd go a variety of places—back to the Casino Room in the Ambassador Hotel in Hollywood or the Flame Restaurant in Phoenix. We had a four-month engagement in Albuquerque at the Hilton Hotel, which was the second hotel that Conrad Hilton had built.

Also, in the early 1960's, I continued to play at other regular stops in Los Angeles. My son John lived there, and it was good to stay connected with him as he was growing up.

And beginning in 1960, every summer found me at the Dunes Hotel in Las Vegas as long as Mr. Riddle, the General Manager, wanted me at the Sultan's Table.

The Sultan's Table

I played solo piano at the elegant Sultan's Table in Las Vegas's Dunes Hotel every summer from 1960 to 1967. I was on a turntable in the middle of the dining room. I wasn't a featured act; I was the live background music as diners were enjoying their meal. The piano went around slowly and the people who were sitting next to the turntable would come within three or four feet of me as I went by.

One of my favorite comedians at that time was Louie Nye, who we had seen first on Steve Allen's television show. His signature line was, "Hi Steverino, I'm Gordon Hathaway from Manhattan."

He had recorded a comedy album that I was aware of long before I even went to Las Vegas. In the routine, he portrays a musician who goes to the bank for a loan. He made his voice sound like a guy that has been drinking too long. His character is named Harold Lips. The banker says, "We cannot give you a loan Mr. Lips, unless you have a job."

"Well, I do have a job," he responds. "Next month, I'm gonna go to Seattle to the Bismarck Hotel where I have a job with Jimmie Lunceford's band."

The loan officer replies, "Well, I am very sorry to have to mention this to you, but Mr. Lunceford has been dead for 17 years."

"He has?" Lips responds incredulously. "No wonder we ain't had a gig lately. I've been blaming it on rock 'n roll!"

He gets on the phone and speaks to Jimmie, only to find out he is indeed no longer living. Well, it probably doesn't play all that funny here, but everyone sure thought it was funny at the time!

Louie Nye was appearing at the Dunes in the main showroom. I had memorized his line about being in Seattle with Jimmie Lunceford's band from a comedy LP. One night, Nye came into the restaurant for dinner.

As I came around him for about the third time, I leaned over and said, "I don't care whether they like me here or not, because I've got a job next month in Seattle with Jimmie Lunceford."

He totally cracked up, and was quite impressed that I knew his routine. Later that night, I gave him the whole routine that he had done years earlier. We became friends and went out during that week he was in town. We went down the Strip to hear Don Rickles and others that were appearing in town. I have always remembered that story, because it was a beautiful set-up. I knew the punch line in the record and it fit my situation when Louie Nye was sitting right there in front of me.

The main attraction in the Sultan's Table was "The Magic Violins from Mexico City." They were thirteen musicians strolling around the room playing beautiful, romantic music.

There were two pianos on the turntable, and both of them were 7-foot grands. They used both pianos. When they went off stage, a waterfall would come on and create a decent sound effect. Then the waterfall would shut off. A spotlight would hit one of the pianos and I would walk out. I would play for about 20 to 25 minutes.

The Magic Violins were the featured attraction, but the people listened and saw me out there. I wore white tie and tails, and patent leather shoes!

Frank Sinatra would come in about once a month or so when he was in town working at the Sands Hotel. As soon as I saw him come in, I would play "Nancy with the Laughing Face." Sinatra recorded this song after some composer friends played it at his daughter's fourth birthday party.

After I played about three notes, his hand would shoot straight up in the air even though he was in a group of about eight guys drinking and talking. He heard the song immediately because he was always listening to the music.

I later read a biography about him and learned that he did not like a restaurant or bar that did not have a piano in it. He loved hearing piano music in the background.

One evening, I ran into him in the hall near the dressing rooms—him and his two bodyguards. He stopped and said how much he enjoyed my playing.

"You're really good. You sound great."

Flustered of course, I said, "Well, you know, thank you very much. Coming from you, I appreciate it. I'm just another guy from New Jersey." It was something stupid like that.

"Well, we Jersey guys gotta stick together," he replied, and he went into the restaurant. That's a moment that I will always remember. In my mind, he was the greatest entertainment star of the 20th century, including movies, music, or anything else. For him to recognize my playing was a real honor.

I found out that Phil Silvers wrote the lyrics for "Nancy With The Laughing Face." Silvers was a famous comedian and played Sgt. Bilko on television. One evening, he was in the Sultan's Table. In that brash Sgt. Bilko voice, he asked me if I knew how to play "The Man I Love." I told him that I did.

"E Flat?" he said.

"Yes," I replied. So, he sat down at the other piano.

"You play the first chord of each bar and I'll play the melody," he said. "Okay, let's go."

So, I go "boom" on the first chord and he sings, "Some day he'll come along..." on the piano. I go boom again on the second chord and he sings, "The Man I Love."

He played the melody and I played the chord changes. He went up and down the keyboard with his arms flailing. Everyone is watching because he's nuts, as you know, and we finished the whole song.

Then he got up, bowed, and went back to his table. "The Man I Love" has never sounded quite right to me since that night!

These experiences were really fun for me, because I was young, and I appreciated these stars paying personal attention to me. Phil Silvers was appearing on Broadway at the time in a show called "Do-Re-Mi" and the main song from that production was a tune called "Make Someone Happy." I played it for him.

One evening Jack Benny came in with a group of men.

On his radio show, his wife, Mary Livingston, would call long distance to her mother who lived in Plainfield, New Jersey. I have no idea why they picked Plainfield as the town where her mother lived. But, Mary called long distance weekly to her mother. It was a running joke on the show because her call annoyed Jack since he was known as such a tightwad.

As I went by his table that evening, I said to him, "I'm from Plainfield, New Jersey."

He looked at me and said, "Never been there," and the turntable moved on.

Liberace often came in for dinner during my time at the Sultan's Table, usually with a group of men including his conductor, Gordon Robinson. I had actually been introduced to Liberace when I was doing *The Orrin Tucker Show* in Hollywood in 1955. One of Orrin's musicians was Lloyd Ulayte. He was also playing trombone on Liberace's afternoon TV show. Lloyd offered to bring me to one of their rehearsals so that I could meet Liberace. When I met him, he was very nice. He said he had seen me on *The Orrin Tucker Show*.

Liberace was a wonderful showman. I did a lot of the stuff that I watched him do. When he was doing the afternoon TV show, however, the only hint of the showmanship was the candelabra on the piano.

Later, when he was doing Las Vegas and Reno floor shows, we saw all the showmanship—the elaborate clothes and the big rings. He would show the audience the ring and say, "You'd better applaud. You paid for it!"

When Liberace came in, I would always go over and visit with him during my intermissions. One time, I told him that my mother was coming out to visit me in Las Vegas from New Jersey. I told him I was going to bring her to see his show.

He said, "Tell me when she is coming, and I will make the reservation." I wasn't surprised by this gesture, because I knew he had been close to his own mother.

When my mom came out, I took her to the Riviera, and we had seats in the first tier. He wowed my mom and she loved the show. Later, I asked for the check, and the waiter said there was no bill since we were guests of Mr. Liberace. I wasn't really surprised that he picked up the tab either, because I figured he was that kind of a guy. In that very show, he introduced Barbra Streisand to the public. That was her first big job as a soloist. She opened the show.

Several days later, Streisand was in the Sultan's Table having dinner. As my piano went past her, I leaned over and said something like, "How does it feel to be the talk of the town?"

"It's a lot of fun," she replied. That was the first and only time I ever talked to her!

For a while, Bobby Sherwood, who was a well-known band leader in the early days, played at The Dunes with a quintet. He played the guitar and the trumpet. Bobby and his wife Phyllis sang. He had real nice quintet and they played in a lounge that was built just for them at the entrance of The Sultan's Table. As you entered the restaurant, you walked through this lounge to get to the main restaurant.

He was a terrific guy. Also, I have to admit that I developed a little crush on his wife, Phyllis.

It was a great time and I guess I was living the high life

of the traveling musician... until the fall of 1963, our regular stop in Dallas, Texas.

Dallas, November 1963

I was downtown in Dallas the day President Kennedy was assassinated. The motorcade passed me at the corner of Harwood Street and Ross Avenue. I was extremely distressed over his assassination. Dallas was called "The City of Hate" at that time. A protestor had assaulted Adlai Stevenson just a short time before Kennedy's visit and the assassination just cemented the image of Dallas as a city of extremists.

I was so depressed that I wanted to get out of Dallas for a while. I decided to return to Japan. Of course, things had changed in Japan in ten years. Now, I had to have permission to work there. Years earlier, while I was playing and booking acts in Yokohama, I got to know a Japanese booking agent in Tokyo.

Tats Nagashima was a brilliant, forward-thinking man. By the 1960's he had become the premier concert promoter in Japan. Tats had promoted every international artist who performed in Japan; from big band musicians like me to other groups you might have heard of like the Beatles, The Rolling Stones, and Michael Jackson.

Tats agreed to make a "dummy" contract for me in which he assumed all responsibility and guaranteed me a certain salary. It was the Japanese equivalent of a "green card." I started going back to Japan in 1965. In fact, I worked in Japan on three-month engagements every year for three years until around the time I decided to permanently settle in Dallas.

Tats sent me to exciting cities in Southeast Asia to do shows for the local citizens and for the American troops stationed nearby. For instance, he booked me in Taiwan twice. I'll always remember taking a train from downtown Taipei to the boondocks in a city called Tainan. It was a good-sized town and we had an airbase there.

One afternoon, I was walking around the area just looking at the surroundings when a girl on a bicycle rode past me. As she passed I heard a screech of bike brakes, and a voice said, "Jack? Is that you?"

Mind you, this was in Tainan, and an American girl thinks she knows me. Well, she sure did. It was Jean Edscorn, with whom I had gone to school from kindergarten through high school.

Her parents and mine were good friends and played bridge together, among other things. It turns out that Jean had become a missionary and had been sent to Taiwan to preach to the locals! I invited her to one of my shows and she took me to a Chinese wedding of one of her congregation. It was quite an experience.

I had a couple of risqué ditties that I did in my show. One of them was about Hawaiian beach boys. Some of the beach boys in Hawaii are huge around the middle, and they are called Kanaka boys. The girl in the ditty was known as Sweet Leilani who had the Biggest Kanakas in Hawaii (as bodyguards). It was funny to the troops.

I would do that ditty for the enlisted men because there were no women present. At the NCO and O-Club shows I didn't do tunes like that because the officers had wives and family with them. Anyway, Jean was a real sport, and she wasn't offended at my show. I had not been sure that I should invite her, but I was glad that I did.

In Manila, Tats sent me out to Clark Air Base, about 50 miles from Manila, and I performed weekends for the EM, NCO, and Officers' Clubs. I remember that the piano at the EM Club at Clark was one of the worst I had ever dared to touch (the officers always had a nice grand).

Well, I looked at this piano, looked out at the guys waiting for the music, had a beer or two, looked at the piano again taking note of the missing keys (and the piano was surely way out of tune), had another beer, sat down, and then pounded out some of the best boogie-woogie I had ever played! The guys went nuts.

To this day, when a client says, "I hope our piano is okay," I think of that night in the Philippines and say, "I know it will be just fine!"

During the week, I booked myself at the Club Alba on Dewey Blvd in Manila. The street name was for Admiral Dewey when I played there, but was later changed to a Philippine hero's name, Jose Rizal. Al Alberts was the headliner. He was the leader of The Four Aces, a pop quartet, but had left the group in 1958 to try to make it as a solo act. In the 1950's, the Four Aces had a bunch of hits; "Love is a Many Splendored Thing," "Stranger in Paradise," "Tell Me Why," and several others. It was fun to open for Al Alberts and to get to know him. We played Clark Air Base together.

At Club Alba, I played with the house band, except for one Valentine's Day.

The Platters were there. The agent that had booked me had also hired The Platters to do a Valentine's Day show.

I had made good friends with the Club Alba owner, Carlos Magdaluyo, so when they were having a special Valentine's Day show, featuring The Platters, he gave me top billing on the neon lights outside. Carlos did not want me to be the opening act for The Platters, because in his mind, I was the big star since I played some Philippine songs, and was his friend.

So, he had The Platters open and I finished. As you can imagine, this didn't set too well with the Platters, and when the show was over, Tony Williams, their lead singer, came up to me and said, "Who do you think you are, taking the billing above us? I'm going to beat the s__ out of you."

I said, "I didn't do it. Mr. Magdaluyo did."

He said, "No, you figured you would take advantage of the fact that they know you here and you were going to be the closing act."

Club Alba's bouncer was Quiel Segovia, an ex-movie star in the Philippines. He had played tough guy parts similar to those played by George Raft and Jimmy Cagney in the early films in the States. Quiel came over and said, "Is everything okay, Jack"?

I said, "Yeah, Tony was upset because they had to open the show."

Quiel turned to Williams and asked, "Is there a problem, Mr. Williams?"

Tony said, "No, everything's cool."

I've had lots of experiences, but the excitement of having Tony Williams of The Platters ready to flatten me was the tops!

I re-visited many of my old stops while I was in

Southeast Asia this time; on my tours through Asia I always used the local musicians to play my background music. What an experience that was! You should see those old arrangements now; covered with Asian music marks and foreign languages.

I played in Hong Kong in a new place called the Blue Sky Ballroom. One of the girls that danced in the line there befriended me and took me around Hong Kong and showed me the sights there.

Tiger Balm Gardens, for example, was a famous amusement park built by the Aw family and named after the Tiger Balm products. She took me to the racetrack where the horses run the other way. In Hong Kong, the horses run to the left!

That's the way it went. I got to know people in every place I went. It was a tough schedule and I loved every minute of it. I was young and single at the time. I had a great time playing with all the Japanese, Filipino, and Chinese Bands.

The Warwick Hotel - Houston

In 1967, the Warwick Hotel in Houston replaced the Dunes as our summer stop. My four-piece combo played the Warwick Club in the famous Warwick Hotel. We did that every summer until the mid-1970's.

In 1968, Major League Baseball's All-Star Game was played at the Astrodome in Houston. The players stayed at the Astroworld Hotel, which was near the Dome. But the executives, the retired great stars of the game, and the owners stayed at the Warwick.

The night before the game, several retired baseball

greats came in for dinner. I saw Joe DiMaggio, Pee Wee Reese, Joe Medwick, and many others. These were the players from my growing-up days of baseball. It was quite a thrill because I love the game so much.

I saw Stan Musial having dinner with his Cardinals teammate Red Schoendienst. I walked to the table to say hello to Stan Musial. He said something like, "Glad to meet you, Jack. Is it all right with you if I play the harmonica with your band?"

What could I say to the great "Stan the Man" Musial of the St. Louis Cardinals (not to be confused with my idol "Stan the Man" Kenton)? I said, "Uh, that would be great."

He came up to the bandstand with a small harmonica, not a big professional model. He took it out of his coat pocket and said, "Red River Valley in F."

"Okay," I said. He played the song perfectly all the way through!

Then he wanted to do "Jimmy Crack Corn." He was going a mile-a-minute on the harmonica and it was actually very good. Everyone saw him on the bandstand and they were all yelling and cheering.

Playing at the Warwick Club—the top society place in Houston at the time—and meeting these wonderful people was another great experience for me and the boys in the band.

Leslie Ann Seright

Two of the regular Friday night members at the Warwick Club were Les and Geneva Seright from League City, near Houston. One evening in the summer of 1968, they came in with a beautiful young woman. So, naturally I went to visit them at the intermission and found they had brought their daughter along. She was a student at LSU and had come home for the summer.

Now, I was 20 years older than any college student by this time, but I was really intrigued with her. Her name was Leslie Ann, and I started a conversation with her at the table.

When I got back to the bandstand, I told the guys, "I just met the greatest looking chick you ever saw."

A week or two later, on a Sunday night when the Warwick Club was dark, I went to Galveston to have dinner. I was cruising around and stopped at the Golden Greek, a popular Galveston restaurant at the time. In the restaurant were Mr. and Mrs. Seright and their daughter Leslie Ann.

Mr. Seright (I was calling him Mr. Seright then) invited me to sit with them. We had dessert and then the four of us went to the Balinese Room where I danced with Leslie Ann.

An old friend named Billy Williams was there with his band playing that night. Billy was a band leader who sang. He was known as "that singin' man." He made "That Old Lamplighter" a hit.

My romance with Leslie Ann began that summer's evening in 1968. Well, to make a long story short, Leslie Ann and I got married in September 1969.

My Itinerant Days Come to an End

Part of the Warwick contract was an apartment for the band leader in the hotel. Of course, my new wife thought that was terrific, living in the world famous Warwick Hotel. When our first daughter, Andrea, was born, we brought her to the apartment. Not long after, our second daughter, Mandy, came along. The days of traveling from Houston to Dallas to Japan for four months at a time came to an end.

But Houston and the Warwick weren't the place for us. Dallas was, with my society patrons, and the Chaparral Club became my home base. I began to make a living in Dallas as a big band leader.

8
Settling in Dallas

MCA Divests its Booking Business

MCA (Music Corporation of America) was very good to me. They kept me busy on quality jobs from the time I signed with them in 1956 until I moved to Dallas in the early 1960's. They're the ones who booked me at the Chaparral Club in Dallas. They were my one and only agent.

MCA as a booking agency finally folded around 1962. Attorney General Robert Kennedy's Justice Department determined that MCA was violating anti-trust laws. MCA was making their own movies, then booking the movies into the theatres they owned, and also hiring their own stars to be in the movies!

As I recall, MCA was given choices as to what they wanted to do, but they could not keep operating as they had in the past. MCA elected to continue to make movies, but to divest itself of the talent agency. The individual agents within MCA formed dozens of agencies themselves, all independent and all with different names.

I had been working in Dallas for a couple years by then, and was known throughout the southwest, so I decided not to sign with a new outfit. I would book myself. In addition, I hired a Dallas booking agent, Phil Brown, to book my society dates. Phil had been Joe Reichman's manager. Phil and I agreed that he would get 15% when he booked my big band for society dates. There were quite a few of those. In fact, I believe I did a dozen or more jobs through Phil the first few weeks that I was a Dallas resident.

Later, I realized that anyone who knows about this kind of music already knows me. So, if they wanted a band that played music of the '30's, '40's, and early '50's, or wanted a band for a wedding, they would know how to find me. I have not had an agent or booking manager in the United States since 1962.

The Permanent Move to Dallas

So with the Chaparral Club as my primary engagement, I was playing private parties, ballrooms, and country clubs. At the time, Texas was full of live music and The Great American Songbook was still popular.

I came to the conclusion in 1968 that Dallas would be a good place for me to settle down and make this my base of operations. So it was primarily a business decision. I met a lot of nice people, but more importantly, Dallas was a place where I could become very well known in the big band business.

Now I say I stopped traveling once my children came along. That isn't completely true. What I did was limit my travels to the southwest, and mainly Texas. I plunged into the debutante social scene in Dallas, Houston, Longview, Wichita Falls, and San Antonio. We would play these beautiful parties—society affairs and ballroom dates. Then we would break up the big band for the fall and play the Chaparral Club with a quartet.

I continued to meet more people, which led to more one-nighter engagements in Texas. I was getting very well known with the Dallas Country Club gang, as many of them were members of the Chaparral Club.

One of the nicest members of the Chaparral Club was Tom Landry, head coach of the Dallas Cowboys NFL team. Both of us began working in Dallas in 1960, the year the Cowboys were organized and the year the Chaparral Club opened. When Tom's daughter Lisa was married, the wedding reception was in Austin at a country club on Lake Travis. It was a beautiful affair, and Tom asked us to play at the reception.

The Best Jewish Band in Town

We also began playing at Jewish social affairs, many of them at The Columbian Club, located in Carrollton, a northern suburb of Dallas. It consisted mainly of Jewish members. This was still a time of ethnic discrimination, especially in the south, so Jewish people had to have their own country club. Since I was a kid from Jersey, where Jewish communities were far larger, I was familiar with a lot of traditional Jewish songs. I played Jewish weddings and other events even as far back as high school.

Still, there were a couple of Jewish members at the Chaparral Club. Howard B. Wolfe was big in the garment industry. One of his daughters was getting married and he asked, "Ever played a Jewish wedding?"

"Yeah, back in Jersey I played plenty of them," I answered.

He wanted to give it a try, and we did.

Then I played for the Donald Zale family, the Lester Melnick family, and Richard Marcus (the son of Dallas retail icon Stanley Marcus). There were Jewish musicians around Dallas, of course, but we managed to get the big weddings because we could play just as well, and could offer that sweet big band sound.

Marshall Head got an album of recordings by Mickey Katz. Mickey Katz was a Jewish comedian and musician who lived in Los Angeles and was well known on the Jewish social circuit in California. He also happened to be Joel Grey's father.

Mickey had a distinctive way of playing the clarinet. Marshall began playing just like Mickey and it was a riot. It would make me think I was back in the catering halls in Brooklyn when he would play "Die Greene Koseene" and other Jewish songs.

Soon we were known as the best Jewish band in town!

The Society Band Business

I wrote about Joe Reichman briefly earlier. Joe Reichman came to Dallas from New York and was playing the top society parties for many years, beginning in the 50's. His home base in Dallas was the Adolphus Hotel.

When I first arrived in 1960, Joe was still very active and so was a band leader named Herman Waldman. Herman's band was well known in the various hotels in Dallas and other major cities in Texas. He had made a name for himself at the Gunter Hotel in San Antonio.

Herman and Joe really welcomed me to Dallas and were both instrumental in helping me get my Dallas union card. In fact, the union rules were much the same as they were back in Los Angeles when Klaus Landsberg and Sterling Way had to vouch for me at the union hall.

In Dallas, I had a 4-month engagement about to begin at the Chaparral and I couldn't wait three months for a union card. Both Joe and Herman told the union that they needed to make me a member immediately, and they did. (Incidentally, we played for Herman Waldman's 80th birthday party at the Columbian Club.)

In the society band business, I was the principal rival of a musician named Mal Fitch. While I called the Chaparral Club my home base, Mal led the house band at the Cipango Club in Dallas. I think we developed this rivalry mainly because the Chaparral Club and the Cipango Club were the top two private clubs in the city. We felt like he did not do dance jobs as well as we did though, so I was able to combine ballroom dance jobs with the society jobs and make a nice living at it full time.

Each of us was kind of figuring that when Joe retired, our band would take over. I was getting into my 30's then... a wily veteran! I had already been playing professionally for 15 or 16 years.

In terms of years, maybe I didn't have a lot of experience. That isn't a real long time in the music business. But by the time I was 30 and playing in Dallas, I could do every style. Whatever you wanted, I could do it. And as you've read, I had been everywhere!

Things were a little bit negative around here for a while because I knew that Mal didn't want me to play here. In fact, I know he opposed my union membership. "We've got rules and regulations," he argued.

Mal is retired now and is living in the piney woods of east Texas the last I heard. He's a few years older than I am, but he developed a hearing problem, which is not good if you're in the music business!

He had this thing going with his bass player, Jerry Roe. When someone came up to the band and made a request, Mal would say, "Sure!" Then he would look up at Jerry and in a few seconds, Jerry would say the name of the song. He could hear what the request was and he would tell Mal after the customer left the piano. (Mal played the piano.) The last couple of years he never heard what a request was, but he could still play it.

I actually saw Mal a few years ago with his wife, Dorothy, and we had a very friendly meeting. As we got older, he and I became pretty good friends. He's friendly now you know, because I'm not a threat to him anymore.

There used to be a real popular bar down on McKinney Street in Dallas called Joe Miller's. Joe Miller was the bartender and owner, and he knew everything about the local music scene.

One night I walked in there and the place was full of people from the local press, Channel 8, and the music business. They were hanging out there in those days. Joe was behind the bar and he said loudly, "Here comes Jack Melick. Mal Fitch taught him everything he knows." Everybody in the room who recognized Fitch's name or mine broke up. Me too. It was very funny.

Of course, Joe Miller is long gone, but having him around in that era was fun. He just proved I was getting known around town outside of the Chaparral Club.

The Social Season

The members at the Chaparral Club were mainly older folks and downtown business people. It cost quite a bit to join the club, so most of the members were established business people for 30 to 40 years. When we played social events, the affairs were elegant.

The Social Season in Dallas kicked off the last Saturday in October with a big dance held by one of the social clubs in Dallas. It might be the Terpsichorean Club or the Calyx Club (both clubs still exist today, by the way). Yep, that's right, the Social Season was an actual season with a start date and end date.

At this big ball, Dallas society would present its debutantes. There were a different number of "debs" every year. Sometimes it was only 6 or 7, and sometimes as many as 12 or 13. The girls were 18 to 22 years of age. There were usually 8 or 10 of these events and we got our share of them. We would get about half of them and Mal Fitch would get the other half.

Whenever I did a wedding or debutante party, I would meet with the bride (or deb) and her mom, sometimes including the grandmother—you know, the one who was paying for the whole thing. We would discuss what music should be played, the presentation song (if it was a debutante party), and so forth. The bride or deb would always question me about mixing in some rock-'n-roll with our music for the younger people.

I would say, "Sorry, we don't do that, but those bands don't try to play 'In the Mood' either!"

Well, sometimes they tried, but it just wasn't the same. But I found a way to co-exist with these new sounds of the 1960's. It's the main reason we're still able to find work even today.

I would suggest they hire our band to play from 8:00 to 11:00 or so while grandma and her friends were there. Then we'd pack up and bring a local rock band to play until 1:00 or as late as the kids wanted. That idea was not my original idea, but it was what was starting to happen.

We did not want to alternate with a rock band because we could never compete with them. Our big band with 11 members would never be as loud as a rock band consisting of 3 or 4 guys and $20,000 worth of sound equipment.

But, I explained that after we finished, we would be happy to turn the stage over to whatever local rock band they wanted. It depended on whether or not the family had the money to pay for two bands, but at the debutante level, they usually did. We played for debutante parties all over the southwest using this "formula." We were so successful with the idea that some society parties took it to the next level.

In the early 70's, the Jack Melick Orchestra played a deb party in Corpus Christi. We were outside on a dance floor the family had built over their swimming pool! They had set up bars out there, and that's where they danced to our dance music. Meanwhile, inside the house, they had cleared out the living room for a rock band to set up.

So, we played outside during a beautiful starlit night with dancers in long gowns and tuxes. More or less on cue at 11:00pm, we hit our last note outside, and inside the house, Chubby Checker and his band struck the first note of "The Twist," and the transition to rock-'n-roll was complete for the rest of the evening. I didn't even mind sharing the evening with him.

In fact, he was very nice and said how proud he was

to be in Corpus Christi playing with Jack Melick! He was still very popular then, and the evening was fine.

The Social Season would end on the last Saturday of January. It ended the same way it started—with another big party at one of the social clubs. The Season was timed this way because the debs were college girls, and they were heading back to school in January.

Most of the deb parties were in Dallas, but we played deb balls every year in Odessa, Wichita Falls, and Longview. During that time, there was still a lot of work for the big bands even though the social events were dying out in the rest of the country. Dallas still had a Social Season.

Slowly that kind of steady work began to come to an end. The social and cultural tastes changed a lot. The Social Season, as we remember it, is almost completely gone now. There are only one or two functions a year now that feature big band music and the old style dance music. We worked seven nights a week for a long time, so when the social scene ended, I was ready for whatever was next.

And the Songbook Begins to Fade...

Most musicians never learn "public relations" and that's why a lot of them don't work very much. But I learned pretty well I think. Over the decades, I made it my business to get to know the "right people." From the Chaparral Club to the Columbian Club to the Dallas Country Club, I got to know everyone.

Around the mid-1950's, the onslaught of rock and roll began. It was the era of youthful rebellion, and we were told that, "This is not your parents' music." That was really the end of the Great American Songbook in my estimation because it was our parents' music. It was the music that brought us together as generations.

The advent of rock-'n-roll was the birth of the generation gap. I know that many people believe it was a difference in political values that caused the break, but I think it was the music.

That wonderful music, the Great American Songbook, started going downhill when Elvis Presley, Bill Haley and those early musicians started to get famous. It was aided in its downward spiral in the '60's when The Beatles came along. It's never recovered. And now, it seems to me, it's as low as it can go with metal, rap, and the shouters and the screamers. It's not even music anymore.

Given music history, and the downward spiral in the quality of music, I've always thought that my greatest accomplishment was not how well I played, nor how good my band sounded! It's that I have found an audience to make a living for almost 70 years playing the kind of music that I have loved and believed in. I still do.

I'm not rich and famous, but I am famous in certain circles... and have lived a comfortable life playing just the kind of music I wanted to play.

You know, I got that degree in public school education at Oberlin College, but I never have taught, in a school or privately. Even if they don't teach in school, many working musicians will supplement their playing income with teaching. But I've never done anything except play the piano and lead the band. Doing that, I have never been involuntarily out of work in almost seventy years.

9
The Beat Still Goes On

Semi-Retirement

I have been semi-retired for about 5 or 6 years now. I realized that I had been playing full-time for over 70 years, so I decided the band would not travel as much as we had in the past. We used to go out some 50 times a year, playing one-nighters and weekends in San Antonio, Austin, Oklahoma City, Tulsa, and so forth. I made the decision that we would cut out a lot of that traveling.

I started a retirement account back in 1974 and it grew quite nicely. I had two mutual funds that were part of my retirement program. Thankfully I had taken all that money out of the market and bought a couple of permanent annuities before the crash in 1995 or 1996.

So, I thought I would use this money to find a place to live. I found this place called Highland Springs in North Dallas. It seemed so great when I first saw it, that I didn't even keep looking around. I took the money out of my retirement accounts to use for the down payment and deposits.

So this is where I moved. It has worked out perfectly. I love the place and I still play as much as I want to. As a matter of fact, in September of 2013, we played a big charity ball here at Highland Springs. It was one of the biggest and most important engagements we have ever played.

Serendipity

What I can say is that I have no regrets regarding my musical career. I have played around the world. I have played solo, small ensemble, and with big bands in many exotic places. I have played in the finest country clubs around the world. I have few bad memories.

There are some sad things that happen in our lives. My sister Jane died in a private plane crash. She was only 35. Gabi, the Las Vegas girlfriend I met when I was working at the Sultan's Table, died in a car crash in 1962 while I was playing in Texas. These two events, although heart-breaking, were out of my control.

So I could never look back on those events, and let them ruin my life. They just happened, just as good things happen. I am blessed to have had way more good things happen to me than bad ones. I would agree that I have been very lucky, all the way. Honestly, it's all been serendipity. It seems like I have always been in the right place at the right time.

When I moved to Dallas it was just the right time because the big band business was crumbling everywhere else. But with the support of a couple of retiring band leaders, a handful of highly influential patrons were looking for a guy like me.

When I was a teenager, it was just the right time because all the older, working musicians were off to war; opening opportunities—like Camp Sagamore—for younger musicians like me that otherwise never would have been there.

While in Korea, it was just the right time when I was playing a piano in an empty room as an aspiring, but apparently influential, young actor named Richard Long happened by. Next thing I know, I'm booking acts in the Far

East instead of fighting in a foxhole.

While I was playing with Leo Peeper's band, it was just the right time because Jimmy Palmer needed a piano player for his band. His schedule caught my eye because they had an upcoming date at the world-famous Palladium.

While we were playing at the Palladium, it was just the right time because the president of KTLA-TV—broadcasters of *Dancetime at the Palladium*—was putting a new music show together and needed a solo pianist.

That show didn't last very long—only 18 months—but it was long enough for MCA, the largest talent agency in the United States, to see me and offer to represent me. It was just the right time for them to send me to Reno, Nevada because the band leader who played the Sky Room on the top of Reno's Mapes Hotel moved across the street. They were looking for a new band leader and there I was.

The Sky Room wasn't open very long, but when it closed I headed home to Los Angeles. It was just the right time, because on a break from a string of engagements with nothing currently on the way, my phone rang at 4:00am. The voice on the other end said, "Jack, this is Guy." Guy Lombardo had just lost his second piano player to an injury. Freddy Martin had recommended me. Did I happen to be available? Wow, was I ever available, and all I needed was a red coat!

Anyway, there's an old saying that it's better to be lucky than good. I hope the people that have heard me over the years think that I'm a little bit of both.

Just as a side note, I have a memory of those two guys (Freddy Martin and Guy Lombardo) when they were in Dallas.

At that time, the musician's union ran a private club called The Artists' Club that was open practically all night. All you had to do was show your union card to get in. It meant anyone in show business—entertainers, bartenders, strip tease dancers, musicians, or comedians—could get in. After work, we would go to this club and there would be jam sessions. Guys would bring their horns and play. It was wonderful. That era was ending right when I got to Dallas, but the club was still there for several years for me to enjoy.

On one extraordinary night, Guy Lombardo was playing at the Music Hall in Dallas, while Freddy Martin's band was playing at the Statler Hotel. That night, I went up to the club after I finished at the Chaparral Club and saw Guy Lombardo and Freddy Martin sitting together.

I had, of course, worked with them both so I sat down. Now, it was Guy Lombardo and Freddy Martin, two iconic legends of the Big Band era, so let's just say that I sat down as humbly as I could. Although it sounds like a self-serving memory now, a conversation ensued that I will never, never forget.

They began to good-naturedly argue about who discovered me first! It was just thrilling, really, because these two famous guys were arguing over someone not so famous (well, except in certain circles). Finally, I had to give the nod to Freddy Martin.

"Well, Freddy, didn't you recommend me to Guy?"

He said, "Yes, I did!"

I never played with his band, but we were at the Ambassador Hotel at the same time. I would have to say that he was the first big name to help me out in California.

And *that* was a conversation I will never forget.

Today's schedule

Now that I am semi-retired, we play for the (much) older ballroom dancing crowd about four or five times a month.

There are several dance clubs I also play for. One of them is the Dallas Dinner Dance Club. They have their parties at various country clubs around the Dallas area. It is largely the money crowd in Dallas. I think it is composed of a hundred couples and they have four parties a year. We play at least one of them, sometimes two.

There is another group called the Trippers Dance Club and they have their dances at the leading country clubs around town. The first time I played for them was in 1968. The last time we played for them, they made a big deal out of how I had been playing for them since 1968. A couple of the dancers were at the first dances in the late 60's.

The Calliope Club of Dallas has about 75 couples that joined together because they like dancing to big band music. They have 3-4 dances a year, usually at top-notch country clubs in the area.

There is also a group like this in Tyler. They are older people, the society leaders in that city. When I first came to Texas, I played at their social club called the Badminton Club. It was formed in the '20's when they actually played badminton.

Another club in Tyler is called the Venetian Club. They are still going strong. We play for their parties in December and May every year. We also play at the Tyler Rose Festival dance. It is a very important event in North Texas.

Even today, when people in the great southwest want a band that can play big band music, they call on Jack Melick.

Only Two Remain

Now, as far as I know, there are only two of us left. The other big band era leader who is still living is Ray Anthony. Ray appears to be still going strong, and he's into his 90's now, about eight years older than me.

He played with Glenn Miller and Jimmy Dorsey and formed his own group after World War II. He was a very young leader. He was most popular in the early '50's, and had a couple of hits including "The Bunny Hop" and "Dancing in the Dark." He's probably most well known as the writer and recorder of the theme music to the iconic TV shows *Dragnet* and *Peter Gunn*. He even has a star on the Hollywood Walk of Fame.

All of the biggest names are playing in that Great Ballroom in the Sky, but Ray Anthony and I are still playing right here in the USA. We met and got to know each other in the Big Band Academy of America.

He now has a business buying and selling albums. He has amassed a catalog of 1,800 to 2,000 big band albums over the years. He buys my CD's for about $6.00 and sells them for $18.50! He does that with everybody. He gives money to the estates of the departed band leaders, but it is his business. He does great.

The Big Band Academy of America

During the '70's, I became a charter member of the

Big Band Academy of America (BBAA). The organization was founded in 1976 in Hollywood.

Up until very recently, I would go to Hollywood every year for their reunions. The Big Band Academy was composed of band leaders and musicians from the big band era, as well as people who simply loved the music. The Big Band Academy ceased to be active in 2013, and is now composed mainly of people who love the big band sound.

The organization was founded by big band author Leo Walker to preserve the history of big bands and jazz. He was the first president. Leo retired in 1986, and Milt Bernhart, who was lead trombonist in Stan Kenton's band, assumed the presidency. Of course, you may remember reading that Bernhart was the one that led us to that unforgettable night in Cleveland back in my Oberlin days.

Milt passed away in 2004, and his son David took over as the BBAA president. The annual reunions have not been held in several years... well, it wouldn't be much of a reunion because Ray Anthony and I are practically the only ones left, but David tries to send out a newsletter every few months to keep lovers of the Great American Songbook informed about big band news.

It's About the People

My greatest kick on the bandstand, or my greatest enjoyment about being the leader, is seeing the reaction of the people. We're not into this to play for ourselves or for our own achievements. We are in it to make the people happy. At least I am, and I'm the leader of the band, so the band members have to feel that way, too, or at least follow my direction and understand why we're doing what we do.

If we start to play and nobody gets up to dance, I have to wonder why. I ask myself, "What's the matter?" I begin to think of tempos and song choices, and I make some switches. Maybe we go into something a little slower... maybe we play more Latin tempoed music... maybe we play more soft background music. We keep doing this until we find exactly what they want. Then we swing through the rest of the night, and the people just have a great time.

Other newer leaders don't know how to do that or they don't even try. But these little circles of big band music lovers, ballroom dancers, and people who remember music from the Great American Songbook... these are my circles, which are ever diminishing as the years go by.

I have reached the stage where I don't have to play anymore if I don't want to. But I will continue to play the Great American Songbook until I am unable to do it.

A Subject of Research

A few years ago, I got an email from a college student in Japan named Shin Aoki who was writing his doctoral dissertation. The subject of his paper was the music that American GI's listened to during the Korean War.

He wanted to know if I was the Jack Melick who had played in Japan from 1951-1954. He had studied the archives of the *Pacific Stars and Stripes* and saw my name quite often in the entertainment section of the paper.

I laughed when I read his email because my best friend in Japan at that time was Al Ricketts, the entertainment editor of the paper, and the guy who wrote all that stuff. Anytime I was playing in Japan, I would tell Al and it would appear in the paper almost immediately.

I continued to correspond with Aoki-san and give him all the knowledge I had of who performed both for Japanese civilians and American troops. I shared with him who was big in Japan at that time, what songs were popular, and other interesting information from that side of the world at that time.

His treatise came out a little while ago. It was written in Japanese. I am still waiting for my copy in English!

Epilogue

People have told me through the years that I am resilient, that I always seem to land on my feet. But as I look back, I failed plenty of times, but I never remember thinking that I'm going to give this up. I never believed that I couldn't do this.

One time when we were playing in Reno, I already had an established band, and the musician's union was running a national contest. This is about 1960, and I was only about 30 years old. The American Federation of Musicians (AFM) was sponsoring an annual contest trying to help bring back the big band business. The objective of the contest was to select the best new band in the country. The prize was a recording contract and six weeks at Roseland Ballroom in New York as I recall.

So we entered in Reno, and competed against three or four bands in that section of the country. We won the sectional contest. The regionals were in San Francisco at the Ali Baba Ballroom. We took the band down to California. The Reno local paid our expenses since we were representing them in the big contest.

There were seven bands in the regionals. We came in dead last. Now, I never thought that this was humiliating. I still thought that as far as "sweet big bands" were concerned, we still had the best in the country.

When I think about it, my attitude was shaped way back in high school when Bill Evans was getting the jobs and I wasn't. He may have been the best thing that ever happened to me. It forced me to evaluate what I do best. I learned that what I do best is play dance music, and communicate with my audience; better than any other band leader that I know of. Today for sure since there aren't that many bands now, and of the bands that do perform, I'm the sole remaining member of the big band era.

What if I had decided to compete with the Bill Evanses of the world? What if I was dead set on trying to play jazz, or being a solo pianist, or fighting to get on *The Ed Sullivan Show* or whatever? What do I do best? My band and I play dance music better than anybody. So I stuck to it.

No doubt in my mind, we played the best dance music in that AFM regional band contest, but the other guys were powerhouses; great soloists, jazz beats. They swung the joint, rocked it. Everybody was focused on the musicians. But when we played... the dance floor was full! And that's what matters most to me.

When it came to voting which is the best band, one of the powerhouse bands from Las Vegas won that year. But I know that they would flop trying to play the places where we played. It's a case of knowing what you *don't* do best, and knowing what you *do*.

Big Band dance music? Yeah... we were the best.

Several Christmases ago, Jack was visiting with the family of his longtime companion, Patsy Eldredge. During the evening, as he was regaling the family with tales of his musical adventures (at their invitation, of course), several of his listeners commented, "You know Jack, you really need to write this stuff down."

"Yeah, everyone keeps telling me that," Jack answered, "but outside of songs, I'm not a writer."

Nick LaVecchia, Patsy's brother-in-law, piped in, "You know, I'm a writer, Jack. What are we waiting for?"

Beginning in the spring of 2011, Jack and Nick began to record hours of interview material about Jack's experiences. Anything Jack could remember was recorded. From 20+ hours of audio recordings, the makings of a memoir emerged.

Nick lives in Parker, Texas. He is the principal in THEWRITEHOUSE, a media production company. He's also a writing teacher, which is probably why it has taken five years to get from a recorder on Jack's dining room table to the book you have in your hands right now.

Nick studied broadcast journalism and production at the University of Florida.

There are no circles in which he is famous.

A musician's life is difficult. Jack always worked mostly fronting his own band. Reno, Vegas, Texas. His children all graduated from college and are successful today...

Jack is traveling and fronting the last of the big bands. And he is helping thousands of older folks remember the good old days while dancing to some beautiful timeless standards and listening to some good music. Some very, very, very good music. When you work hard and have good friends, it all adds up.

Jack usually got the girls, but I got the laughs. You tell me which is better.

from the Foreword by Jim MacGeorge

COVER IMAGES: (FRONT) JACK AT THE SULTAN'S TABLE RESTAURANT, LAS VEGAS, 1966. (BACK) THE JACK MELICK SHOW PERFORMERS, YOKOHAMA, JAPAN, 1953. JACK WITH COMEDIAN JIM MACGEORGE AND THE KOBAYASHI SISTERS.

$15.00
ISBN 978-0-9974085-0-8
51500>
9 780997 408508